Few Choices: Women, Work and Family

Network Foundation for Educational Publishing
is a voluntary foundation set up:

1. To facilitate the development of a healthy and responsible Canadian-controlled post-secondary book publishing sector.

2. To assist in the production, dissemination and popularizing of innovative texts and other educational materials for people at all levels of learning.

3. To develop more varied sources for critical works in the Humanities and Social Sciences.

4. To expand the readership for Canadian academic works beyond a select body of scholars.

5. To encourage the academic community to create books on Canadian topics for the community at large.

6. To develop works that will contribute to public information and debate on issues of historical and contemporary concern, thereby improving standards of education and public participation.

The Network Basics Series, one of the Foundation's activities, provides inexpensive books on the leading edge of research and debate to students and the general public.

This Network Basic is published by Garamond Press. Please direct all enquiries to 67 A Portland Street, Toronto, Ontario M5V 2M9.

Few Choices:
Women, Work and Family

Ann Duffy, Nancy Mandell, Norene Pupo

Garamond Press
Toronto, Ontario
A Network Basics Book

A publication of Garamond Press

Garamond Press
67A Portland Street
Toronto, Ontario M5V 2M9

Typesetting: Coach House Press, Toronto

Printed and bound in Canada

Canadian Cataloguing in Publication Data

```
Duffy, Ann Doris
   Few choices

(Network basics series)
Bibliography: p.
ISBN 0-920059-64-3

1. Women -- Employment.  2. Work and family.
I. Mandell, Nancy.  II. Pupo, Norene Julie,
III. Title.  IV. Series.

HD6053.D84 1989        331.4        C89-094302-8
```

Contents

Preface

We would like to thank the many individuals who contributed their time and effort to this project. We were fortunate to have the assistance of skilled interviewers – Theresa Chubak, Vida Preece, Stacey Levine, Anthony Sylvestre, Rod Swain and Rose Hutchens – and we thank them for the enthusiasm and care they brought to their work. Rose Hutchens provided much more than her exceptional skills as an interviewer and we would like to thank her for the time, energy and insights she so generously provided. Our thanks also to Dusky Lee Smith, who kindly agreed to edit part of the manuscript, and to editors Gilda Mekler and Irit Shimrat. Reviewers Hugh Armstrong and Harriet Rosenberg provided feedback and valuable suggestions that were most helpful in writing the final draft.

Our appreciation is extended, particularly, to the many women who took time out of their busy days to answer our questions: thank you for the information and insights that you so kindly shared.

Needless to say, our families contributed directly and indirectly to our labours. We thank them for their support and understanding, and for the inspiration they occasionally provided.

Finally, we very much appreciate the unwavering encouragement provided by Peter Saunders and Garamond Press.

Note: The authors are listed alphabetically. Each author contributed equally to the manuscript.

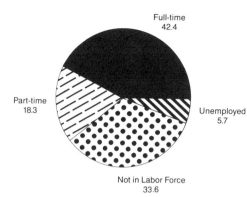

Full-time
42.4

Part-time
18.3

Unemployed
5.7

Not in Labor Force
33.6

Statistics Canada, December 1987: 96-97
Canadian women with employed spouses who
have children under 16 years of age.

CHAPTER 1

Women's Work and Family Patterns: Constraints and Options

Canadian women are in the midst of tremendous change in their work and family lives. The ever-rising number of married, employed women and the steady decline in the birth rate are signs of this revolution. The way women's decisions about work and family are intermingled reflects the prevailing interpenetration of domestic and wage labour under advanced capitalism. Drawing upon the actual experiences of individuals, we explore both the difficulties women encounter, and the coping strategies they devise, as their lives become more and more conditioned by paid employment. By focusing on a range of women's employment patterns – full-time paid work, part-time paid work and full-time, unpaid domestic work – we reveal the complex, diverse, and competing ways in which domestic and paid work intersect.

Central to our theoretical understanding of the position of women in contemporary capitalist society is our explanation of the forces that shape women's ways of dealing with work and family commitments. The experiences of our respondents reveal how women's decisions about bearing and rearing children interact with their work goals, and how these decisions emerge from the women's social contexts. Each woman's decision reflects her independent assessment of what seems to her the most suitable course of action within a structurally constrained and narrow range of possible alternatives. We explore the meaning and consequences of these alternatives by elucidating the forces that precipitate women's actual decisions, and by allowing the women to assess their own courses of action.

Work and Family Patterns in Transition

For much of this century, what marriage and childbirth meant to Canadian women was a lifelong commitment to unpaid domestic labour. In 1900, the majority of women in the paid labour force were young – between fifteen and 24 years of age – and single. Marriage and children meant withdrawal or expulsion from paid employment. In 1931, only 3.5 percent of all married women engaged in paid labour. Even at mid-century, only 10 percent of married women were paid workers (Wilson, 1986:75-98; Phillips and Phillips, 1983:1-51).

The lives of most mothers were centred on home and family. Adult life was presented to women as a predictable and orderly path, with clearly marked signposts of progress and success. Children were to be prepared for school, guided through adolescence and then launched into families of their own. Homes were to be created, sustained and improved. Husbands were to be supported and encouraged. Although real life frequently failed to live up to this ideal, the expectations were clear, and were passed on from one generation of women to the next.

In the last three decades, the structure of women's lives has been almost completely reformulated. Paid employment now increasingly dominates many women's adult lives, just as it does men's. The traditional family, with a working father and stay-at-home mother, is becoming less common; this description now applies to approximately 24 percent of Canadian families (Boyd, 1988:87). Even the transitional pattern of postponing paid employment until the children are older, or until they are in school, is being steadily eroded. Between 1975 and 1983, labour force participation increased by 14 percent for women whose youngest child was between six and fifteen years old; 16 percent for women whose youngest child was between three and five years old; and 17 percent for women with at least one child under three years old (Statistics Canada, 1985:4-5). Today, 66 percent of women with employed husbands and children under age sixteen work for pay. Approximately 60 percent of employed women have employed husbands and preschool children, or children less than three years old (Statistics Canada, 1987a:96-97). As a result of these changes, contemporary mothers are having to develop new ways to negotiate the intersection between family, work and self.

The increased involvement of married women in paid employment reflects major changes in the social structure; transformations in the labour market and the nature of paid work; rising inflation; and changing attitudes about women's capabilities, responsibilities and needs. Since 1950, the increased demand for clerical workers, the proliferation of service jobs – notably in health and education – the expansion of sales work – especially in the retail trade – and the need for cheap, peripheral labour in the manufacturing and textile industries have created many jobs for women (Armstrong, 1984). At the same time, high levels of unemployment among both men and women, labour market uncertainty, unrelenting inflation, and the steady erosion of wages have forced more and more families to intensify their wage-earning by means of wives seeking paid employment or husbands taking on second jobs. These economic pressures have been accompanied by changes in family life, including improved birth control, the increased accessibility of divorce, and the ideological support for women's employment provided by the women's movement.

Mothers' Lives Today

At present, Canadian mothers face three alternative employment paths, which can be followed individually or in sequence. The traditional pattern typical of 1950s' women – that of working full-time as a mother and homemaker – is becoming increasingly uncommon. Few modern families are still insulated from women's paid work experiences. Only one-third, or 33.6 percent, of married women with employed spouses and children under sixteen are currently neither employed nor (officially) looking for work (Statistics Canada, 1987a). And the relatively few women who direct their energies solely to home and family do so for shorter and shorter periods.

The prevalence of the second employment alternative – the combination of domestic responsibilities and part-time work – has increased markedly. About one-fifth (18.3 percent) of women with employed husbands, and children under sixteen, work part-time for pay. Women make up the overwhelming majority – almost 72 percent – of the one in seven employed people who work part-time. In all, 25.3 percent of employed women (compared to 7.6 percent of employed men) work part-time (Statistics Canada, 1988). Women who work part-time are more likely to be married and to have children than women who work full-time (Wallace, 1983:45-52). About one-quarter of employed married women work part-time. Approximately one-third of these women have preschool children.

Of all the employment alternatives, by far the most common for Canadian mothers is full-time employment. Slightly more than two-fifths, or 42.5 percent, of married women with children under sixteen work full-time for pay (Statistics Canada, 1987a). And, for the more than one million women who are divorced or widowed, or who have never married, regular employment has always been a necessity.

Each of the three employment paths affects women and their family relationships differently. In this book, we compare and contrast these paths in order to reveal the day-to-day realities entailed in each. In particular, we are concerned with three principal sets of questions.

First, how do women come to pursue a particular employment

pattern? What factors draw women towards, or away from, domesticity? How significant are women's early ambitions, their initial work histories, their partners' expectations, their financial worries and their children's demands in determining the extent of their participation in the paid labour force?

A complex variety of public and private interests interact to pull women into particular combinations of work and family. Personal considerations – such as number and ages of children – are influenced by, and interact with, such societal considerations as the availability of affordable childcare. Ultimately, women's work and family patterns reflect an interaction between socially structured opportunities and constraints, and active attempts to make sense of and respond to such conditions (Gerson, 1985:192).

In their day-to-day lives, women experience constraints and opportunities that curtail the range of their options. Pursuing one option limits other possibilities. Trade-offs are thus built into the structure of options for women. Moreover, since women experience work and family demands as contradictory and competing interests, choices in one sphere often depend on the opportunities, incentives and constraints of the other. Throughout this book, then, we discuss the ways in which social arrangements structure women's choices. In particular, we note how employment opportunities, childcare responsibilities, the feasibility of living on a husband's wages, and the perceived benefits and constraints of domesticity profoundly influence women's work and family patterns.

Second, we examine how women, once launched on a particular track, manage their day-to-day lives. Each employment alternative entails a particular set of rewards and costs. The intersection of the private and the public is played out in the delicate juggling act women perform in satisfying their personal needs within the structure of advanced capitalism. The organization of the labour market creates and reinforces the conditions under which women are exploited as unpaid workers at home and as paid workers in the labour force (1985:26). In the domestic sphere, women provide services that are necessary for the survival of the family unit, whatever its particular form. In the public sphere, women's labour is generally rewarded with lower wages, less prestige and fewer opportunities for advancement than is men's labour. Despite the massive movement of women into the labour force, it is still the domestic role that is seen to define women (Oakley, 1974).

It is true that many women spend less of their lives bearing and rearing children than was common in the nineteenth century and more of their lives working for pay outside the home. But under patriarchy – a male dominated society – women's family obligations are generally seen to take precedence over their employment responsibilities. In both concrete and ideological terms, the structure of advanced capitalism maintains women's economic, social, political and psychological dependence upon men. How do women experience their work and family choices? How do they decide between and resolve competing interests? How do they actively resist stereotypical depictions?

Our final line of inquiry seeks to ascertain how mothers articulate and evaluate their own lives. Recognizing that we are looking at a particular group of women at a certain moment in their lives, we explore the ways in which these women account for their situations and assess the impact of their present circumstances on their personal and work relationships. Most recognize that their actual choices (as distinct from fears or hopes) depend on the balance of gains and losses circumscribed by their social context (Gerson, 1985:96). Only some aspects of women's behaviour can be explained as a function of societal coercion. Others must be understood as women's active attempts to create their own lives based on their personal preferences and social positions, and their interests as they perceive them. To stress only external coercion in the form of capitalism and male dominance is to underestimate women's involvement in creating their own lives. In contrast, a totally phenomenological account overemphasizes the ability of individuals to shape their futures. What is required is an interpretive framework that takes into account both structural forces and individual negotiation. Surely the tension between these forces – a central sociological problem – is that to which Marx referred when he suggested that "Men [and women] make history," but not under conditions of their own choosing.

A Note on Methodology
This book draws on women's accounts of their own lives. Its intent is to provide an evaluation of women's decision-making processes and an assessment of the personal and public consequences of their decisions, as seen through the eyes of a sample of women currently experiencing changes in their patterns of combining employment and domestic responsibilities. We purposely study married women between the ages of 25 and 50, because statistics suggest that these are the women most likely to be undergoing such changes. Further, since we assumed that childless married women face problems somewhat similar to those of childless married men, we restricted our sample to women who have custody and / or prime responsibility for at least one child under sixteen.

In Chapter Two, Nancy Mandell focuses on the problems and delights experienced by married mothers who work full-time for pay as they juggle their multiple responsibilities. Mandell's interpretation comes from data derived from questionnaires administered to 59 full-time workers in North York, and in-depth interviews with 33 women from the same area. Both of Mandell's samples are randomly derived, and hence represent a range of class and ethnicity.

In Chapter Three, Ann Duffy presents the full-time housewife's perspective. Duffy's analysis is based on in-depth interviews conducted with 30 housewives from Metropolitan Toronto and the Niagara Region. The broad range of income levels, ethnic and cultural differences, and variations in family size, household organization and husbands' occupation, represented in this snowball sample capture diverse demographic characteristics. (In snowball sampling, interviewees are asked to suggest other interview subjects.) While noting their diversity, Duffy highlights the striking similarities in these women's lives.

In Chapter Four, Norene Pupo looks at married women who work part-time, each of whom has at least one dependent child. Using snowball sampling, Pupo draws on interviews conducted with 50 women in the Metropolitan Toronto area, most of whom are employed in those economic sectors and occupations that have seen the greatest growth in part-time work in the last decade. This chapter provides insight into the similarities in the paid work experiences and in the household strategies of these women, despite the women's diverse backgrounds.

The women surveyed come from many ethnic and cultural backgrounds. But, although members of visible minorities are represented here, their number is small. In this sense, our samples do not adequately reflect the heterogeneity of Canadian society. For example, the experiences of Native women or women from Third World countries may not be sufficiently reflected in our results.

We caution the reader to treat this material as suggestive of sociological trends; it is not meant to be representative of Canadian patterns, and cannot necessarily be generalized to apply to other communities. These predominantly urban samples do not address the question of regional diversity. It may also be that, as Metropolitan Toronto or Southern Ontario residents, the women interviewed are subject to housing and food costs that make household economics a more constant pressure here than elsewhere in Canada. In addition, we recognize the methodological problems inherent in our decision to use three different samples as a basis for comparison in this book.

Offsetting these limitations is the quality of data we present. Although there is now considerable quantitative data in North America documenting the double day, there are few in-depth studies presenting rich detail on women's day-to-day struggles. Nor are there many intensive examinations of the lives of full-time mothers and housewives. Too often this group is demeaned and rendered sociologically invisible. As for part-time workers, they are often unjustly stereotyped as not having enough commitment to pursue a career. In all three cases, we hope to reclaim and re-envision women's lives by giving women a forum in which to voice their perspectives.

Our methodology, and specifically, our use of in-depth interviews, reflects our appreciation of the concerns of feminist methodologists about traditional social science research. We share their preference for "soft" rather than "hard" (or survey) methods. We attempt here to avoid the pitfalls of traditional social science research methodology – particularly its separation of subject and object, its construction from within an ideological framework that maintains an imbalance of power between researchers and others, and its contribution to sociology's practice of gatekeeping (Smith, 1974). Rejecting the traditional perspective of sociology – a view seen from above and at a distance – we have regarded the interview process as an "interactive exchange" (Oakley, 1981), in which we tried to link our own experiences with those described by the women we interviewed, in order to more fully appreciate and describe the realities of women's lives (Cook and Fonow, 1986). This meant that, in conducting interviews, we had to know when, how and whether to ask particular questions, when to pause for reflection, when to share thoughts, and how to interpret expressions and experiences (Pupo and Duffy, 1987). Our purpose was to avoid imposing definitions of reality on these women and building barriers between them and us. We hope not only that this presentation allows women an opportunity to discuss these alternatives, but also that reflections arising from such discussions will precipitate change in personal decisions and structural arrangements.

Conceptualizing
We are not content to present excerpts of our interview data within a theoretical vacuum. Rather, we have focused our presentation and interpretation on the concept of choice. In this book, the word "choice" refers to actual decisions that women can make in balancing work and family commitments. On the one hand, external, societal forces facilitate or constrain women's possibilities. On the other hand, within a limited range of often contradictory options, women make personal decisions based on what they perceive as their best interests. That women often interpret their choices ambivalently reflects the inherently contradictory nature of our society, which pits family demands against work options.

The terms "choice" and "decision-making process" imply a straightforward selection between possible alternatives. In fact, work and family decisions rarely come quickly or easily to women. Often, a long, drawn-out process takes place in which a woman, step by step, becomes committed to a course of action. The succession of her commitments constitutes a career path. The suggestion by functionalists that early childhood socialization experiences determine adult behaviour is not borne out by our interviews. Parental ideals and aspirations may serve as normative benchmarks for adult behaviour, but, taken alone, they are poor predictors of adult development (Gerson, 1985:65). Nor do societal conditions – such as the availability of daycare, equal pay, jobs and financial security – entirely determine a woman's future. These conditions, however, certainly shape women's perceptions of their options. The alternatives available are certainly similar within groups of women of the same age and marital status, who have the same number of children of the same ages. What differentiates women within these groups is the sequence of their work and family commitments, which, in a period of between ten and 20 years, reveals a distinct pattern.

In reviewing the interview material and hearing these women describe the dilemma of having to balance the demands of motherhood and family life with the strains of the workplace, we, as academics, mothers and women, identified with their stories. More than once during the preparation of this manuscript, each of us found herself caught between workplace problems and family predicaments. Sometimes her course of action was clear. Family or personal matters took precedence over workplace concerns, or *vice versa*. Sometimes the answer was harder to find. Whatever the circumstances, there were few real alternatives. We hope that this book will help stimulate discussion and, ultimately, efforts that contribute to a greater range of choices, and more opportunities for women to make real decisions.

Full-time
42.4

CHAPTER 2

Juggling the Load: Mothers who Work Full-Time for Pay

Introduction

Expectation and Reality: How did women get where they are?

Since industrialization, the belief has existed that family and work exist as separate worlds that operate independently of each other (Kanter, 1977). The development of industrial capitalism in Canada has brought about the physical separation of the private realm of family intimacy from the public experience of labour that is largely responsible for the academic treatment of work and family as distinct and noncomparable areas of study. Recently, scholars have criticized this approach and argued for an analysis that considers the interaction of work and family.

Both work and family are "greedy institutions" (Coser, 1974) that make simultaneous demands on women's emotional energy, physical strength and intellect. Family life shapes the nature of people's work experience, just as employment affects families (Crouter, 1984). As Hertz (1986) suggests, all marriages are shaped by work. Work determines a family's standard of living. For the individual female employee, the demands of work spill over into family life, shaping the ways in which she manages her domestic and childcare responsibilities. For example, inflexible work schedules and heavy time commitments constrain women's daily household management, and determine their need for paid and unpaid help as well as the quality and quantity of the time they spend with their children.

Women's family choices also limit and shape their work commitments. A woman cannot devote endless hours and energy to work if she has children (especially preschoolers), lives with a partner who also has to work hard, and has little discretionary income.

This study explores the fumbling, tension, joy and strain experienced by mothers who have full-time jobs, as they attempt to juggle their multiple responsibilities.

Which Women Work?

Approximately 60 to 75 percent of all women between the ages of 20 and 54 are employed. Most adult Canadian women earn some income from employment. In 1987, approximately 57 percent of married women participated in the labour force (Statistics Canada, 1987a:87). As shown in Chapter One, today's women are far more likely to continue working with the advent of marriage and children than were the women of any previous era.

The drop in real incomes in the past five years reinforces the need for more women to work for longer periods, and to continue working even when their children are preschoolers. Most Canadian women now look forward to a lifelong combination of work and family roles. Ninety-five percent of Canadians marry at least once in their lives; almost 60 percent of married women hold either part-time or full-time jobs; and almost 90 percent of married couples have at least one child. Few young women now assume housekeeping and childcare as a primary, permanent occupation. And few married men still expect to be exempt from domestic duties on the grounds of supporting their families financially. Many couples now share the roles of breadwinner and household / child manager for most of their married lives. This shift from traditional, hierarchical, gender-role-segregated activities to relatively equal, shared, gender-role-integrated relationships has caused confusion, ambivalence and tension in Canadian marriages. Not having grown up with role models they can now emulate, and receiving little institutional support from their work environments, most spouses are bewildered by the demands of dual-earner households.

Although more women are now working, the types of jobs they hold, their remuneration relative to men's, and their opportunities for occupational mobility have not changed much. Women's work is characterized by occupational segregation and pink-collar ghettos. Women are relegated to poorly paid jobs with poor working conditions and little security, stability, or opportunity for advancement. In 1983, 77 percent of all female employees in Canada worked in one of five occupational groups: clerical (32.6 percent), service (18.6 percent), sales (10.4 percent), medicine and health (9.2 percent) and teaching (6.2 percent) (Wilson, 1986).

Despite media stereotypes of working women as highly paid

professionals, briefcases firmly in hand as they fly off to exotic locations, only 7.4 percent of employed women in Canada hold professional or managerial positions. The demands and benefits of integrating work and family are very different for these women than they are for working-class women. Although professional women may work long hours in taxing jobs, their relatively high salaries allow them to purchase domestic, personal and family services that considerably ease their load. In addition, their jobs confer high self-esteem and a sense of competence quite different from the feelings of alienation, boredom and being unappreciated that stem from repetitive and highly supervised labour (Rinehart, 1987).

Yet, despite dissimilarities between their working conditions, and despite the enormous income differential separating working- and middle-class mothers, their lives are similar in many ways.

Part One of this chapter presents women's definitions of their current lives, tracing their career development, their movement into full-time employment and marriage, and their attachments to both these aspects of their lives. Part Two outlines the problems and delights experienced by married mothers who work full-time. All the quotations in this chapter are from mothers who work full-time, but many of the perspectives found here can also be found among full-time homemakers, and among mothers who work part-time for pay. These perspectives reflect the experiences and expectations of women in our society.

Methodology
The data in this chapter come from two sources. One is in-depth interviews with 33 women between the ages of 25 and 47 who were employed full-time in the labour force. Each woman was interviewed in her home for at least two hours. The interview schedule was open-ended, and designed to elicit the women's perspectives on the effects of full-time employment on their family lives. The second source of data is an extensive questionnaire administered to 59 mothers who work full-time.

Both samples were chosen from one community in North York that Census Canada identified as having a broad range of income levels and a high proportion of families with dependent children. This deliberate sampling procedure ensured a wide range of class and ethnicity representative of the population – Toronto mothers who work full-time for pay. The questionnaire sample contains a high proportion of dual-earner families earning a combined income between $30,000 and $75,000 a year. Many of our questionnaire respondents either work in middle-level business in jobs traditionally held by women, or hold adequately paid positions in the manufacturing or service sector. Most have not completed high school. In contrast, the interviewees are better educated; most have some university education. They are also better paid, having business, academic, or professional careers. Ethnically, the interview group is predominantly white, and includes Catholics, Jews and Protestants. Questionnaire group members are much more ethnically diverse; many are immigrant women from Europe and Asia. One-third are Black women from Canada or the West Indies. Each of the women interviewed is married, living with a partner and caring for at least one child under thirteen. Most of those who received the questionnaire have children. One quarter of the women in this group are single parents; one-eighth are not married to their live-in partners.

In conclusion, the interview group is more typical than the questionnaire group of the well-educated, relatively affluent, young and upwardly mobile group often stereotyped by the media as "super-women." The questionnaire group members more closely resemble the average Canadian mother, who struggles to maintain a decent standard of living for her children and is likely to take a retraining program to improve her employment status.

Part One: Early Work Histories

Why Women Work

Money motivates most women to work and guarantees their continued employment. It also creates tremendous tension within marriages. In his analysis of the family life of employed Toronto women, Michelson (1985) found that 70 percent of his respondents said that money motivated them to work. Sixty-eight percent of the full-timers and 49 percent of the part-timers mentioned financial need as a motivating factor. Michelson's findings are consistent with other Canadian data (Luxton, 1980) that cite income as a precipitant of employment. Family income is inversely proportional to married women's rate of participation in the labour force.

In short, women work for the same reasons men have always worked – because they need money to survive. In Chapter Three, which discusses full-time housewives, we see that income predicts employment, but does not always do so consistently. There are, for example, non-employed mothers in low-income families who cite their preference for full-time mothering over wage labour. Despite a growing body of sociological literature exploring various motives for women's employment, income statistics consistently reveal that financial necessity predominates. Women of all ages, regardless of their marital status, work not by choice, but because they assume sole financial responsibility for themselves and their dependents, or because their partners' incomes are not high enough to maintain a decent standard of living. Only the most privileged women in our society can actually choose whether they wish to work.

Yet the belief that women's work represents a voluntary decision prevails in our society, in part because the ideology of mothering emphasizes women as mothers, not as workers. As adolescents, the women of today were socialized to put their desires and goals for mothering ahead of career goals. They spent most of their time marketing themselves as smart, beautiful wives and mothers, rather than as intelligent and able workers.

The strategy women used up until the 1970s – guaranteeing their financial future by marrying well – was more appropriate in an era when married women had few opportunities to work for wages. Even though, historically, most men have never been able to earn enough to completely support their dependents, married women supplemented and stretched the family budget through means other than wages. Some, for example, raised vegetables or eggs for the table or for sale, or made clothing.

Today, being provided for by a man is still a popular aspiration (Baker, 1985), but an increasingly unrealistic one, whose results for young women may be financially disastrous. Women continue to curtail their education and career planning in order to bear and raise children. Yet many spend a significant proportion of their lives as sole supporters. For example, almost one of every ten Canadian families is headed by a single mother. These women often lack the resources to earn a decent living (Statistics Canada, 1985).

The Transitional Generation
The vast majority of women interviewed here characterize their paid employment as involuntary, permanent, contingent and unplanned. These women's work and family lives are at odds with their adolescent ideals. This is the baby-boom generation: women born between 1945 and 1960. Raised during the 1950s and 1960s, they aspired to follow in the footsteps of mothers who were full-time homemakers. They now seem quite perplexed by the radical disjuncture between their childhood aspirations and adult realities. They are profoundly ambivalent about their desire to combine full-time employment with mothering, and about the effects of their double employment on their family lives, their children's behaviour and their spousal relationships. Throughout our interviews, women express surprise about the course their lives have taken, and genuine astonishment at their own competence, intelligence and success in juggling their many responsibilities.

Growing Up
Contrasting their adolescent expectations of marriage and motherhood with their current involvement in full-time jobs, these women demolish the assumption that paid employment is a choice. Their childhood

experiences and adolescent expectations, as well as their parents' aspirations for them, were consistently traditional. Not one grew up in a
nontraditional family where egalitarian parental roles existed. Few
were encouraged to plan for and actively pursue independent lives.
Most were raised in an atmosphere of rigid, gender-role-hierarchical
family roles and relationships.

Nine of the 33 women see their childhood homes as pseudo-
egalitarian (Mandell, 1989): both parents were strong influences, pushing their daughters to be financially self-supporting, educationally successful, and strong and independent in their thinking:

> My father was really very forward-thinking, because he
> thought a woman should have an education and be able to stand
> on her own. He thought [you] should be able to support your-
> self, whether you're a man or a woman.

They encouraged their daughters to obtain professional credentials,
even when the girls proved remarkably resistant:

> My father was a strong influence. He was a high school princi-
> pal and he pushed us – there was never any question that we
> were all going to university. And I remember I was thinking of
> nursing and he was pressuring me to be a doctor. He did pro-
> pose the idea of graduate work in nursing as well, and I scoffed
> at that.

This woman explains that her resistance to further education stemmed
from her belief that, as a future mother and itinerant worker, she would
not have any need for postgraduate degrees:

> I have to admit my idea of nursing was that I would get the
> degree and get married – not necessarily in that order – work for
> a few years, have babies, and then work part-time, and [the
> degree[would be a nice thing to fall back on.

Some women speak eloquently of positive, active female role models,
even though most were raised, at least in their early years, by breadwin-
ning fathers and stay-at-home mothers. They describe their mothers as
"strong, aggressive" women who "always worked [at home]" and were
"quite independent." They saw their mothers undertake heavy domestic burdens, often including the care of four or more children, without
the financial ability to hire help or buy labour-saving devices. They grew
up respecting women's diligence, strength, creativity and energy.

As adults, they have applied these traits to their pursuit of full-time employment and mothering.

Either a mother's active display of female independence, or the persistent urging of at least one parent, seems to have been enough to encourage these women to construct realistic, concrete and ambitious plans for their future. One respondent, reflecting on the effects of determined, consistent parental expectations, comments on how peculiar it was for young girls to have definite, long-range career plans:

> This sounds odd, but I always had a sense of where I should be going, even as a child. Where does it come from? My parents encouraged me to work hard at school and achieve good grades. I was always setting goals and I've always tended to go for great success. And I hoped that I'd marry one day. My father counselled me. He was a crystal ball gazer. He said, "Don't rely on some man for your future."

No doubt there are respondents whose parents feel that they too encouraged their children, only to have their daughters forget or ignore their admonitions. But in focusing only on what adults remember from their childhood, we see two influences emerge: clear future plans, and strong role models.

The majority of our interviewees were raised in homes in which their mothers did not work for wages, or worked only when their children had finished high school. They hypothesize that their parents could have benefited from the wife's additional earnings during the early years of marriage, but the cult of domesticity suggested that women could not successfully combine mothering and working. As one respondent explained:

> It was during the 1950s, and there was all the propaganda about women and their responsibility to stay in the home with their families.

This respondent's mother now runs her late husband's business!

Canadian statistics from the 1940s, 1950s and 1960s show that few married women earned wages. Our sample's description of the traditional mother's career follows a well-known pattern: marriage at the age of 23 or so, to a man two to three years older; childbearing in the twenties, with an average of 3.4 children spaced a few years apart; during the thirties, full-time mothering, possibly combined with unpaid outside interests – such as volunteer work – for middle-class women, and indirect wage-earning – such as babysitting – for working-class women; and a return to paid employment once the children passed adolescence.

All but two of the respondents characterize their mothers as hard workers: energetic, capable, "determined, stubborn and opinionated" women who lived satisfying and demanding lives. Some retain a strong impression of the relentlessly arduous nature of woman's work. One reflects on her Irish Catholic mother-in-law's strenuous life:

> There was not that much money. There were seven kids; it was just baby after baby after baby. So if you want to talk about woman's work – I suffer the strain [of combining work and mothering] in my head, but my back has never been broken and my hands have never been raw with sores.

Even those women whose parents' finances necessitated their mothers' employment refer to their parents' roles as traditional. Some of their mothers had to shoulder the burden of both earning money and "keeping the family together" through periods of husbands' sporadic employment, chronic and violent alcoholism, or frequent absences from home. Interestingly, not one of our respondents, regardless of her parents' means – and despite current Canadian media, literary and cultural depictions of 1950s' homemakers – characterized her mother as idle, frivolous, lazy, helpless, or subservient.

Deviation from traditional scripts caused our respondents' parents confusion and marital strife. Wives tormented husbands unable to fulfill the role of breadwinner. Until the mid-1970s, an employed wife symbolized her husband's failure to provide adequately for his family:

> My father wasn't doing very well. Whenever he did work, he didn't make the living that was necessary. My father was a furniture salesman, and then he took ill. And the hospital bills were incredible. Even to this day, my mother puts him down like a mouse. She always degraded him because he didn't make money.

And husbands attempted to constrain wives to a narrow enactment of the domestic role.

How do our interviewees assess their mothers' commitments? We heard both praise and condemnation, but the median response was a mixed review. Our respondents recognize that domestic ideology limited their mothers' work opportunities. Many recall childhood security and contentment with their stay-at-home moms, but decry the price their mothers eventually paid. One social science graduate student expresses the ingratitude, pain and humiliation older women can experience:

My mother-in-law didn't work; she was a homebody. And now her husband has left her after 35 years, so she has to try to get some skills and go out to work, which is almost impossible at her age: she must be about 50. And she has no training at all. She devoted her whole life to her two sons and her husband. Her two sons have moved away, she's in Calgary, and now her husband has left her. And she didn't cultivate any friendships.

Many of our interviews reveal the pervasiveness of male marital norms, which condition women's experience of marriage and motherhood. The traditional package of subtle, yet penetrating, cultural blueprints for behaviour includes prescriptions for dress, appearance, and public presentation of self, as well as lifelong restrictions on a woman's use of time and space. Women relate to their husbands and families and assess their marriages in ways that stem from an implicit acceptance of paternalistic definitions of appropriate behaviour. It is often not until late in life that they realize that adhering to all these male norms systematically disadvantages women, both economically and emotionally.

Respondents' Perceptions of Parental Aspirations
The Horatio Alger myth suggests that, with enough effort, talent and will, anyone can succeed. Many of our interviewees articulate their parents' acceptance of this liberal, meritocratic creed by noting their parents' emphasis on children "bettering themselves" through educational achievement. The desire for children's upward class mobility and for their financial and academic security appears to be a universal parental aspiration, cutting across all classes. Each of our interviewees talks of her parents' desire and pressure for "the next generation to do better." One, whose father was an alcoholic janitor, recalls:

From day one, or my earliest memories of it, I [could] do anything and always was encouraged to do everything, academic [things] as well.

She became the first one in her extended family to attend university. The family was both proud of and intimidated by her.

Yet the drive for educational achievement did not obviate the acceptance of traditional gender scripts. Parents' educational aspirations for their daughters were vague and abstract. The daughters were expected to be educationally successful as adolescents, and yet to imitate their mothers' traditional role in the home. These contradictory demands were sometimes revealed to the adolescent daughters by people outside the family. School guidance counsellors, for example, are often not fondly remembered. As one bright, achievement-oriented nurse recalls:

> I was very interested in health care when I was fifteen or sixteen. I wanted to be a pediatrician, and the guidance teacher said to me, "But don't you want to get married?" And I said, "Yes." And he asked, "Don't you want to have babies?" And I said, "Yes." And he said, "It's going to take you far too long, and you want to stay home with your kids."

With what perceptions of their future skills, successes and lives do women emerge from adolescence? Which of the aspirations of their parents (and of significant others) have they assimilated? Do they perceive any contradictions in the expectations of their families, their peers and society at large?

Young women enter adulthood profoundly ambivalent about their occupational goals, unsure of their intelligence and capability, confused about their ability to manage employment and parenting, and confined to short-term planning. Despite their parents' fervent desire for their future success, very few of our respondents acquired, in their twenties, credentials or skills that would lead to financial independence. Rather, they accumulated a diverse bundle of educational skills and on-site training as contingencies, "to fall back on" in those rare periods during which they expected to be economically self-reliant.

Early Marriage and Work Histories

Women's educational and job histories, like many men's, are itinerant and contingent. Women seem to drift through the early years of their adulthood without any firm occupational goals. The women in this study characterize their employment as an unanticipated necessity, difficult to reconcile with their adolescent expectations of full-time mothering and marriage. Says a 30-year-old graduate student in sociology:

> I drifted through my life, absolutely. I drifted into the courses I took. I had no idea what I was going to do. Then [as a young adult] I was involved with a series of men, and I followed them — I still did that with my husband. I went where they were, at great sacrifice to myself. My era wasn't liberated in terms of thinking of having a career. I think I was very confused. I would say, with hindsight, that my emotional relationships clearly took precedence over ambition, and I think they still do.

Asked about their life plans at age eighteen, these women repeatedly cite the traditional mother-and-wife role. Most entertained what one of them describes as a "very narrow vision of what it was possible for me to do." The vision included a primary commitment to marriage and motherhood, with jobs having only a secondary significance. A 38-year-old nurse reflects:

> I don't know if I had any plans, really. Actually, I thought some-where along the line I would probably get married, work for a couple of years and then stay home, like everybody else seemed to be doing. You know, with nursing you can always get a part-time job.

This traditional, "Leave it to Beaver" image, as one woman described it, of the "lovely home, family and children, and mother dressed in pearls" was romanticized as the ultimate goal for young women.

Dreams of pursuing a traditional role meant that young girls' visions of careers did not stretch past marriage and childbirth. One woman contrasts her own short-term planning with her husband's long-range, self-centered, goal-oriented thinking:

> I've never had any long-range plans. My husband had a much more long-range one. He saw his life, I think, in front of him, whereas I didn't. I'm not terribly future-oriented, even today.

Although most of these women's early plans appear to have been short-term, itinerant, contingent and vague, there were notable excep-tions. Some say they always knew where they were headed and that their lives have unfolded, in the words of one, "almost as if I had a mas-ter plan." A few express early and continued disdain for childrearing, even though some succumbed to ideological pressure and went on to have children of their own. As one caustically comments:

> I never thought marriage would be too terrific. I thought being a mother would be horrendous. I was right on both counts.

Most, however, had no goals beyond, or in addition to, mothering. Says one, a graduate student, "I don't think I planned out a career, and I can't ever remember choosing."

Other studies (Hertz, 1986; Luxton, 1980; Rubin, 1976) have high-lighted the high priority both working- and middle-class women accord mothering. Work before marriage is treated as a temporary occupation, filling a woman's time until her "real" job of mothering begins. Our findings confirm this trend; both the consequences of "drifting" and the degree to which it pervades women's thinking in their middle and late adult years, have become painfully obvious to us. It is because we consider this passive phenomenon so hazardous to women's social, economic and physical well-being that we take the opportunity to elaborate on it here.

By "drifting," we mean women's tendency to allow extraneous events and significant others to make major life decisions for them. Both self-legitimation and control of their lives come late to women. Experiences such as falling in love, having babies and assuming the domestic role gradually enmesh women in a web of relationships in which they serve, facilitate and accommodate others.

Living through others seems inevitable for most women since, from early adulthood, they relinquish the possibility of self-centred decision-making and allow their life choices to be dictated by others. Most often, this passive behaviour appears so natural and inevitable as to be construed as an active choice. The ideology of romantic love in the twentieth century justifies all the restrictions husbands impose on wives, and the services they demand in the name of devotion (Reynaud, 1983).

Young girls learn early the hidden messages of the heterosexual love relationship. Wives are expected to show their love by placing their husbands' needs above their own, to facilitate their husband's careers, and to demonstrate their selfless devotion in countless ways. No wonder many of our respondents felt they had no choice in determining their future. Asked to reflect on her educational aspirations, one woman laments her early indecision:

> If I had taken charge when I was 20 of what I was doing, even in terms of graduate school – I went where my husband could get a fellowship. If I had just pursued my career without any encumbrances at all, I definitely would have had degrees from better universities and a better position [as a professor] now. But I never chose; I always followed.

Numerous other respondents describe their early job and academic histories as having evolved in accommodation to the desires of significant men in their lives. One gave up her tenured university professorship in one city to follow her husband's economically insecure move to another city. Another gave up elementary teaching, a move that effectively ended her early career, in order to follow her boyfriend to another city, where she ended up as a waitress. Many quit steady jobs, interrupted promising new careers and had babies they didn't want, all in the name of love. The more they gave up to obtain marriage and motherhood, the more deeply they became committed to sustaining their domestic achievements. All these acts are presented as free choices willingly pursued by women: women are often held responsible for the choices they are perceived to have. Yet, when their actions are interpreted within a traditional gender-role framework, in which women are raised to feel subordinate to men and are discouraged from independent achievement, it is not surprising that women cling to men. What is surprising is that some women manage to break free of these normative prescriptions. One woman comments on the transference of her dependency from father to husband:

> Suddenly, there I was in marriage and, soon after, [I had] a child, and all of a sudden I had to make all these choices and decisions, and I just transferred this role to my husband. Three years later, he said to me, "Look, I can't be your father, brother, husband, lover. You've got to grow up and you've got to start to do things on your own. You've got to find your own friends. I can't be your whole life. I can't push you into things."

Socialized to be dependent, adoring and demonstrably less intelligent than their mates, women succeed in getting married, only to discover that the very traits that made them marketable and desirable are handicaps in managing husbands, children and careers. Women's initial attempts to take charge of their future are confused and uncertain. Having defined their ambitions and the pursuit of their goals contingently – according to the demands of their personal lives – women find it socially and psychologically threatening to plan independently, without regard to the needs and demands of others.

The word "drifting" implies a lack of purposefulness – a kind of aimless wandering through youth – that stereotypes women as idle and useless. This does not describe our respondents, whose energy, intelligence and creativity are impressive. "Drifting," then, connotes for us, a passive passage through life in service to others. In Part Two of this chapter, we examine how, in mid-life, many women re-channel this energy into assuming some direct control of their lives.

Part Two: Exhausted or Exhilarated

How do mothers who work full-time for wages juggle their multiple responsibilities? How do they balance the spheres of work and family to achieve credibility, satisfaction and success in both?

Our respondents spend a significant amount of time discussing role conflicts, experiences of chronic fatigue, and lack of time in which to rejuvenate themselves. But they also relate creative coping strategies from which they derive considerable strength and satisfaction. They assess the effects of their double days on their relationships with spouses, children, co-workers and friends. They evaluate their lives in comparison with those of full-time homemakers and mothers who work part-time for pay, citing the strengths and weaknesses of their "choices."

Throughout this telling, the themes of juggling, balancing, coping and surviving emerge as central. Every one of the respondents expresses astonishment at finding herself performing, simultaneously, the dual role of homemaker and employee. Every woman chronicles the tremendous effort she expends in managing both these roles success-fully. We, too, are amazed, sympathetic, and proud of their struggles. By offering an account of their day-to-day lives, we hope to debunk the "superwoman" image, and facilitate dialogue about the changes needed, both in the workplace and in the family, to accommodate the dual-earner relationship.

Most of our respondents have been combining work and family roles for some time. They are aware of both the inherent strains in dual-earner families, and the concrete benefits of two incomes, a higher stan-dard of living and a sense of efficacy. What conflicts do these women experience in the workplace and at home, and how do they cope?

Role conflict results when pressures from the work and family domains are mutually incompatible in some respect (Greenhaus and Beutell, 1985). Structurally and psychologically, the dual-earner lifestyle is out of sync with the patterns, social structure and mores that support conventional family living (Skinner, 1984). Doing a good job at work is characterized as incompatible with being a good parent. In fact, some mothers who work full-time for pay believe that it is impossible to be both a good worker and a good mother.

Although our respondents do not echo these sentiments, they adhere to a traditional view of both work and family that is still popular today. Many women worry about whether they are neglecting their chil-dren and potentially rearing social misfits because they have opted to allow surrogate childcare. Moreover, many women handle this guilt by maintaining conventional elements within their homes.

An analysis of the typical North American dual-earner household reveals its traditionalism. These families remain essentially gender-segregated, with men assuming most of the responsibility for wage labour and women assuming primary responsibility for household and childcare duties. On average, husbands start their jobs earlier in the day and end them later than do wives, work more hours per week and more days per week at wage labour, more often hold second jobs, and contrib-ute approximately 60 percent of the total family income (Staines and Pleck, 1983). Their work schedules are potentially detrimental to their participation in family life (Bernardo, Shehan and Leslie, 1987). In contrast, employed women spend more time with their children and on housework than employed men, and experience more conflict between work and family, especially in scheduling (Staines and Pleck, 1983). Although husbands of employed wives do somewhat more housework and childcare than those whose wives do not work for wages, they contribute considerably less than their wives do.

Given their different responsibilities, it is not surprising that husbands and wives should experience role conflict differently. One of the most significant predictors of strain in balancing work and family is the total number of hours both husband and wife spend working each week. But men and women are affected differently. Women experience more interference between the demands of family and those of their own work as their husbands' work-time increases; women's work-time does not affect their husbands in the same way. Married, employed women contribute between 28 and 40 percent of total family income, assume primary responsibility for domestic labour and bear the brunt of the problems of the dual-earner household.

It is well documented that parenthood constitutes a physical, psychological and financial stress for both husbands and wives (Miller and Myers-Walls, 1983). Wage labour engenders another set of personal and marital crises. Combining the two seems potentially explosive. Pleck, Staines and Long (1980) report that one-third of all married workers with children under eighteen years of age experience significant stress in balancing work and family.

Our respondents often use physical metaphors to describe the inherent strain of juggling multiple responsibilities. In referring to themselves, they use such terms as "being pulled in several different directions," "always running off and doing the next thing," and "swimming the backstroke away from work and the frontstroke towards my husband and children." Says one:

> Sometimes I'm doing a little bit of this and a little bit of that but not doing anything well enough. You know, I would certainly say about the kids that I'm sort of running after the train but I never get on it.

Many feel emotionally harassed, physically stretched and psychologically fragmented. Although there is no indication that they are not performing well in all their tasks, the constant pressure leaves them no time for reflection and self-assessment. They interpret their performances as rushed and possibly inadequate.

Yet they do not believe that their husbands see themselves the same way. These mothers assume that childrearing and housework are their responsibilities, even though they are employed full-time. As one of our respondents summarizes, they are "old type women caught in a new situation." Many are in their late twenties and early thirties, and were raised with traditional gender-role scripts and standards, which they are now trying to apply to a very different way of living. Their husbands, however, still seem to see these traditional mores as appropriate guides for behaviour. The respondent quoted above describes the emotional difficulties faced by women "caught in the middle between an old dream and a new reality" (Hertz, 1986):

> One doesn't make the old socialization go away by saying, well, now I can be equal and I can divide up the tasks of parenting and household. It's still very different for men and women. You can divide up all the tasks in the world, but the feeling of responsibility of every working mother I know is vastly different [from that of] her working husband. I mean, I don't know any man who would call home to see what's doing with the babysitter. You know, the men walk out the door and that's the end. But for the mothers, there's a sense of responsibility and there are different levels of guilt.

Traditional assumptions permeate most employed mothers' interpretations of the balance they have struck, leaving them with no role model or yardstick with which to measure the changes in their lives. Structural barriers in the labour force serve to further distinguish women's experience of work from their partners'.

Employment Strains

Work stressors emerge from both the structure of the workplace itself and the demands of the way society structures employment. Simply by engaging in wage labour, people encounter occupational demands the fulfilment of which often conflicts with traditional family life. Common to all types of workers is the constant pressure brought on by the need for wages. Chronic stressors include long work-hours, take-home work and take-home worries. Despite the notion that work and family can be neatly separated, problems at work inevitably condition the nature of family life. For example, the scheduling and coordinating problems inherent in managing two jobs as well as children cause spouses continual tension and anxiety. More intermittent, but equally demoralizing to family life, is the stress of unemployment and subsequent job-seeking.

Literature on dual-earner families differentiates between careers and jobs, implying that the former are whole-hearted, professional commitments to a particular lifestyle, while the latter represent semiprofessional involvements in the secondary labour market. In the last ten years, women have begun to enter the professions in greater numbers than before. Yet the majority of married women who work are still relegated to low-status, low-paying jobs.

Much attention is paid to executive stress. But, in fact, low-status jobs often have more inherently stressful working conditions than do high-status ones. First, such positions are often insecure. Even in unionized jobs – which appear to ensure job tenure – corporate takeovers, fluctuating market demands and economic recessions cause the loss of many jobs. Second, many low-status jobs increasingly lack flexibility, and do not give the worker autonomy or personal control over the work. Numerous studies have demonstrated that flexible hours contribute to a person's sense of job and marital satisfaction. A high degree of control over work scheduling leads to less spillover into family life. Finally, low-status jobs frequently entail nonstandard work patterns – such as weekend work, shift work and variable work-days – that disrupt workers' family lives (Gramling and Forsyth, 1987).

Some respondents feel that women's jobs are particularly stressful because they are modelled on traditional, passive scripts for women. Women workers are expected "to obey," "to be deferential to the men," to be passive, docile and nonassertive. Says a mother who also works as a nurse:

> The hardest thing in my job is being in a woman's profession where there is oppression.

Nevertheless, high-level professional women are not free from stress; like working-class women, they find the burden of the double day extremely onerous. In addition to having to overcome gender stereotypes, they endure heavy work demands – including long hours, job transfers, business travel and entertainment, and weekend work – all of which are incompatible with current institutional arrangements of childcare, schooling and family relationships. Professional jobs, geared to a man's lifestyle, assume that all workers are independent, free, and able to devote themselves totally to corporate demands. Such an implicit contract presumes the existence of a full-time caretaker looking after children and home. Given that only one-third of married women are full-time homemakers in Canada (Statistics Canada, 1987a), this is clearly an outdated assumption.

Family Strains
Role overload has been identified as the major contributor to feelings of strain for employed mothers (Rapoport and Rapoport, 1976; Skinner,

1984). When both spouses are actively engaged in work and family roles, the total volume of their activities is considerably greater than that of a conventional, single-earner family (Skinner, 1984:262). Time pressures associated with one role make it physically impossible to comply with the expectations of another (Greenhaus and Beutell, 1985). It is not surprising that our respondents cite distressing strains on their time and energy. Energy is relatively elastic, but time is not, so employed mothers find themselves with very little free time. Women who work 35 hours a week for pay, and who have young children, average another 35 hours on housework and childcare[1] (Berk, 1985). They have less sleep and less leisure time than their husbands.

Some of these strains can be alleviated, but others are structural, flowing inevitably from the interpenetration of wage labour and domestic work. The strain on a married woman varies according to her personal housekeeping standards, whether she has children, whether outside help is available, and whether household tasks are allocated to other family members. It also depends on her partner's career: what stage it has reached, how specialized it is, and how involved he is in it (Fox and Hesse-Biber, 1984).

Raising children is undoubtedly women's most time-consuming and fatiguing enterprise. Parenthood brings on a series of physical, psychological and financial concerns that persist throughout the childrearing period. The physical fatigue of 24-hour surveillance of preschoolers wears down even the sturdiest of women. Many echo this respondent's comments:

> When the baby was two and three, there was a lot of running back and forth and travelling here and there. And of course, it's just tiring to have a child that age, and a certain amount of waking in the night still, which can throw you off the next day. It was a very, very intense time.

Psychological stresses include worrying about children's emotional, physical, social and intellectual development. The ways in which parents and children define and measure each other's successes and failures, for example, often cause conflict.

Parenting problems change during the life cycle. Certainly once children sleep through the night, go to school all day and no longer require full-time care, the frenetic pace slows down. But adolescents present equally troublesome demands. As one woman explains, you cannot purchase every service needed, and this is particularly evident in raising teenagers.

Despite prevalent ideas to the contrary, mothers of older children report that they do not have enough time to themselves, and look forward to their children's independence. Since children usually interrupt mothers more readily than they do fathers, mothers typically report never having more than ten unbroken minutes at any stage of childrearing.

For employed mothers of small children, securing adequate childcare is one of the most distressing problems. In 1984, 52 percent of mothers with a child under three, 57 percent of mothers whose youngest child was between three and five, and 64 percent of women with school-aged children were in the labour force (Cooke, 1986:8). In 1984, some 1.3 million children between the ages of six and twelve required supervision before or after school and during holidays or teacher-training days. Daycare is both costly and difficult to secure.

The Cooke Report (1986) documented the scarcity of quality daycare. Even though licensing and training systems exist throughout Canada, formal licensed centres have spaces for fewer than 9 percent of children whose parents work or study at least 20 hours a week (1986:165). Therefore, most Canadian children are cared for by family members or informal caregivers. Parents must arrange care on their own. In 1982, families in which the mother was employed full-time spent an average of $1,637 on daycare (1986:14). In Toronto, daycare expenses virtually double the cost of raising a child (1986:15). Moreover, under current federal income tax restrictions, parents can claim a maximum daycare deduction from their taxable income of only $2,000 for each child under fourteen years of age. Daycare is still not fully recognized in tax law as a legitimate business expense, despite the fact that most mothers work.

A second major tension in women's lives is money. Precarious job markets and financial insecurity plagues our respondents. Many have the perennial problem of never having enough money to feed their children, or to pay rent and hydro bills at the end of the month. Poverty is rapidly becoming feminized: in Canada, more than one million children live below the poverty line, and 47 percent of all families headed by women live in poverty. Women who have been on Family Benefits see such "assistance" as a psychological and financial trap that infuriates and demoralizes. One respondent explains:

> You want a way to screw yourself? You just have to be on Family Benefits. If you want a really fast lesson in how to lie, cheat and steal, need social assistance. You'll learn in a hurry, boy!

She goes on to describe how women get trapped between their need for state aid, and the failure of Work Incentives and Family Benefits programs to provide the practical help they need to acquire skills and become financially independent:

Work Incentives is another program [government] blows the horn about a lot, which is very little better and in some ways worse than Family Benefits. I mean, it's propaganda, pure and simple. It is not set up to help women at all, to help families at all or to get people back into the work force. What it does is, it dumps you in a minimally paying job, with no future, for two years – a minor support system – and then it leaves you high and dry. I mean, it stinks, too. I get really angry about this.

Professional women's concerns about quality daycare and time for personal leisure seem frivolous compared to many women's struggles for survival. Inadequate housing, nutritionally substandard diets and lack of consistent childcare create debilitating instability and fear.

Domestic labour emerged from the interviews as a third area of stress, since it remains primarily the responsibility of women, regardless of their employment status. This is characteristic of neotraditional roles (Paloma and Garland, 1971), in which both the husband and wife can work "if they wish," but the husband's work comes first in terms of amount of money earned, family influence, and location of family residence. The wife may work, but only if she is capable of holding down two jobs (Mandell, 1987).

Time-budget studies reveal an inequitable division of household labour. When a married mother takes on full-time employment, she increases her weekly work-load by 50 percent; no corresponding shift takes place in her husband's work-load. The wife works about 70 hours a week, although she reduces the number of hours she spends on domestic labour each week from 50 to 28. The time her husband spends on household work increases – to eight hours a week. Thus his relative contribution remains low, and when he does participate, he is likely to see his contribution not as his own primary task, but as voluntary help to his wife. And when he increases his household involvement, he tends to become involved with pleasant childcare tasks, such as playing with or walking the baby, rather than undertaking the children's demanding physical care.

Parental demands for children's participation in domestic labour no doubt increase when mothers assume full-time employment, although these demands vary by class. Children's domestic participation remains grossly understudied; however, early studies (Cogle and Tasker, 1982; White and Brinkerhoff, 1981) report that more than 90 percent of all children more than nine years old perform regular chores an average of four hours a week. Children's involvement in household chores begins when they assume the responsibility of making their own beds, cleaning up their rooms and picking up their toys. By age ten, most children have moved beyond self-centered chores and are doing work for the family, such as setting the table, folding clothes and caring for younger siblings (White and Brinkerhoff, 1981). Children's participation increases with age; girls participate more than boys at all ages. Children whose mothers are full-time homemakers have the highest level of participation (91 percent) followed closely by children of full-time employed mothers (88 percent) and children whose mothers worked part-time (76 percent) (Cogle and Tasker, 1982). The role of children in dual-earner families in Canada, the expectations their parents and siblings have for them, and their own marital and job expectations all remain unknown. Yet we can hypothesize that, in the future, children will increasingly be asked to assume a more involved, independent and egalitarian role within their families. It also seems likely that they will aspire to parental roles considerably less traditional those with which their parents grew up.

Another aspect of motherhood that women find exhausting and energy-depleting is the "emotional work" (Hochschild, 1975) inherent in monitoring, coordinating and managing the lives of others. Mothers' vitality is drained not only by the physical labour involved in carrying out two jobs, but also by the emotional strain of being continually responsive to others. One of our respondents told us that she often fantasizes about being single again, returning home after work able to enjoy silence, solitude and freedom from the domestic commitments that envelop her child-crowded life.

Mothers are constantly "on call" to answer the demands of children and spouses. Having to organize everyone else's life – arranging for others' lessons, appointments, carpools, peer visits, camps and daycare – drains them of their privacy, their leisure time – indeed, of their interest in arranging activities for themselves. Often lacking any physical space of their own in their homes, and daily experiencing an emotional drain, many of our respondents describe such burn-out symptoms as chronic fatigue, depression, apathy, irritability and anxiety.

Many psychologists have characterized women's orientation as connectedness with others (Gilligan, 1982; Miller, 1976). Gilligan (1982) posits a type of female morality that she calls the "web," which emphasizes the fulfilment of responsibilities to others, whereas masculine morality consists of adhering to a hierarchical, presumably rational and abstract set of rights and rules. Emotional relationships with kin, friends and co-workers sustain our respondents through difficult times. In allowing them to explain the ways in which their connections with others define the boundaries of their lives, we have come to appreciate the power of intimacy in these women's lives. Yet the relationships that sustain them can also be experienced as oppressive. As "kin keepers" (Rosenthal, 1982), women assume the role of regulator, overseer and caretaker, physically and emotionally caring for their partners, children, siblings and parents. The need to care for aging parents often occurs in mid-life, when occupational and family demands are heaviest. Children require 24-hour surveillance for years. Friendships cannot survive without emotional investments. "Sometimes," says one woman, "I find just too many people I should respond to."

Accustomed to giving of their time and energy, accommodating others' schedules and putting others' needs before their own, our respondents find themselves drowning in a sea of obligations as their role expands to include the needs of co-workers and bosses.

> Everyone else's needs seem to be more important than mine right now, and they all cut into my work-time.

Ironically, these women, who see intimate relationships – and particularly friendships with other women – as providing most of their social support, become entangled in an ever-expanding web of interdependencies that deprives them of the time they need to engage in such associations.

Coping with Motherhood and Full-Time Employment
Our respondents have evolved various ways to lighten their double loads. Among their strategies for structural role redefinition (Dyk, 1987) are: changing the definition of their role by giving up or adding a particular aspect of the role (dropping a course; making decisions about having babies); soliciting support from others (getting children and husband to help with domestic chores; coordinating childcare with neighbours); and hiring help (engaging a house cleaner, getting teenagers to babysit). Women may also change or reduce their loads by redefining their personal roles. They may set priorities (by postponing certain tasks, ranking activities with "to do" lists, or sharing or delegating work); compartmentalize their lives (by separating work and home life); or reduce the standards of role expectations (by cleaning the house superficially or not reading everything on the reading list).

All our respondents have had to learn time-management skills. Says one professional:

> I've become very efficient, and it's amazing how I've just let things go. I've learned how to really utilize secretarial help to the full; I've learned not to worry about different things. I've just streamlined. But there's the problem, because I realize how close to the edge I am. Because I've streamlined my life to a terrifying level of efficiency.

Other women describe strategies reminiscent of managerial efficiency studies. Daily priority or "to do" lists help women rank tasks in order of importance and differentiate between the urgent and the important. Such lists are useful in separating short- and long-term priorities, eliciting help from others, scheduling tasks in concert with others, and distinguishing between (and appropriately scheduling) interruptible and non-interruptible projects (1987). After experiencing long periods of conflict stemming from role overload, women who cope successfully have learned to anticipate most of the strains they experience, and to develop flexible pre-planning strategies for avoiding overload during peak periods. However, these women generally find their roles far more onerous than they anticipate, and coping skills may only be acquired after the crisis has passed. Furthermore, the process of learning to delegate responsibility to others and to refuse certain tasks often proves inimical to traditional gender scripts.

Many of our respondents echo this woman's statement:

> My most difficult thing in life is saying no to people. I tend to overextend myself and I have to live with the results of that. I would love to be able to withdraw and have a room of my own – I mean in the real, "Virginia Woolf" sense – in fact, to have some privacy.

Most find "saying no" extremely difficult:

> It's been a very hard lesson for me to learn to say no to people – to say, "I'm tired today," or "I don't feel like making dinner," or, "I need to be comforted," or "I need help."

Psychologists suggest that, in order to maintain satisfactory mental health, a person needs at least one tranquil hour every day in which to relax and rest. Yet most of our respondents lack both personal space and time, and few enjoy an hour of privacy every day. One, asked how she manages to get some time off, confesses to hiding in the bathtub:

> I get no breaks. A bath. I look forward to having a bath in the evening, 20 minutes just for me. Twenty minutes I'm not doing anything for anyone else. Sometimes I feel that I don't have enough affection to give to anybody. I guess it's because of trying to meet the demands of everyone else in the family.

Most of our respondents, as previously mentioned, cited money as one of their worst problems. Obviously, women who earn enough can use money to purchase services that considerably ease the burdens of their double load. And family income level affects children's lives profoundly. When family incomes rise, women are able to buy cars, which lessens the enormous amount of time they spend on public transportation travelling to daycare, work, shopping and errands. Higher incomes allow women to purchase adequate childcare. Discretionary income also allows women to purchase household help in the form of mechanical aids (dishwashers, microwave ovens, washing machines), as well as periodic cleaning and maintenance help and fast food services.

The common factor in all the coping strategies revealed in the literature and practised by our respondents is that they are essentially personal solutions, arranged by each woman to lessen her own load. Women's domestic strategies reflect their belief that they alone are responsible for home management. This individual approach to coping (Fox and Hesse-Biber, 1984) is based on traditional values and attitudes about work and family, which assume that a couple must conform to the traditional model, regardless of the costs involved. Women take on the primary responsibility for this accommodation, by such means as having fewer children, waiting longer to have children, choosing less onerous career paths and settling for fewer achievements. But a structuralist approach to this problem suggests that the basic structure of work should be altered, so that institutions could offer alternative scheduling and thus provide greater flexibility for both women and men. Job-sharing, extended maternity leave, part-time work and work-based daycare are a beginning; but they are far from universally available, and only partially meet people's needs. If domestic and work responsibilities are ever to be equitably distributed between husbands and wives, structural solutions must be adopted.

Evaluating Women's "Choices"

How do the women in our study – mothers who work full-time for pay – evaluate their lives? How do we, as authors, assess their "choices"?

The benefits of working should not be overlooked. It is obvious that our respondents' lives are frenetic and chaotic, but they are also invigorating, stimulating, rewarding and, often, enjoyable. Asked what they like about combining full-time paid work with motherhood, they comment on their sense of personal competency and efficacy. Their sense of mastery, not evident in descriptions of their early work and family lives, emerges strongly when they speak of their middle years. Women acquire a voice of their own in gaining control of their career paths and developing experience in managing home and work. Most of our respondents, except those in precarious financial predicaments, exude independence, confidence and autonomy. Most have developed a perspective on their lives that allows them to assess their choices as worthwhile. Their future concerns and plans primarily focus on achieving an integrated balance that will allow them more time and space to pursue individual activities.

Of all their accomplishments, our respondents cite financial freedom as primary. Most revel in the knowledge that they can support themselves and their children. Moreover, their husbands enjoy being relieved of sole responsibility for financial support. As one woman says:

> My husband never had any particular interest in my staying home. Quite the contrary. I think he found early on that sharing the financial burden was a big load off his shoulders, for one thing. It gives him the freedom to not stay with something if he doesn't want to. He can just take off in another direction, both financially and psychologically.

Employment may have another significant effect on women's lives. Women's traditional socialization, which leads to low self-esteem and a strong wish to get married and remain married, predisposes them to tolerate violent abuse from their male partners. One study suggests that two-thirds of all married women experience violence at the hands of their husbands at least once (Roy, 1980). In Canada, although estimates vary, experts agree that at least one in ten women is a victim of wife assault (MacLeod, 1980); this suggests that almost one million women in Canada are battered each year (MacLeod, 1987). At least one-third of abusive husbands batter their children as well as their wives (Walker, 1979). It is thought that women put up with abuse from men because they have been taught from an early age to passively accept what life gives them (Sinclair, 1985). As Sinclair argues in her report on wife assault in Canada, a woman is socialized to assume a "dependent, helpless, childlike stance in the world while the men in her life make decisions affecting her future" (1985:25). The MacLeod Report on wife battering (1987:21) notes that most of the women who stayed in transition houses in 1985 had little education, had small children, and were not working for pay when they came to the shelters. Although it would be simplistic to see full-time employment as a panacea for abuse, our interviews demonstrate that work gives women a sense of psychological competency and economic self-sufficiency that allows them to resist abusive relationships.

We found little evidence of truly egalitarian marriages, in which both partners share power and responsibilities equally. But we did find quasi-egalitarian marriages, in which some sharing occurred. Women in these relationships revealed a degree of marital satisfaction consistent with the literature, which posits a positive and direct correlation between role-sharing and marital satisfaction. Egalitarian couples are likely to report greater marital happiness than others, as a result of their delight and efficacy in fulfilling, but not being overburdened by, both work and family responsibilities.

Many of our respondents, though stressed, assessed the strain as a temporary and necessary investment in their future. Interestingly, in many studies, mothers who are married and employed score higher on all indices of well-being than homemakers. Married career women with children report feeling less depressed or ill in response to stress than others (Kessler and McRae, 1982; Canadian Mental Health Association, 1987). Despite the popular notion that women who try to do too much are bound to face serious consequences, involvement in multiple roles has a positive effect on women's sense of mastery and pleasure (Baruch, Barnett and Rivers, 1983). Our respondents may feel stressed in their twenties and thirties. But by the time they reach their forties, their investment in their jobs has begun to pay off, just as family demands lessen. So while they experience significant "hassles," they also derive considerable emotional benefits from their increased self-esteem and enhanced support and social networks.

Women who combine wage and domestic labour often find that the time of intense career-building coincides with that of raising young children, which puts heavy demands on a couple's time and energy. A common response is to put the marital relationship on hold, investing instead in work and children:

> We didn't have much time for each other because we were really concerned about the children, because they were quite young, maybe two or three. I was trying to survive and he was starting a whole new job, a new career, so we spent a lot of time together as a family but he and I certainly neglected our time with one another.

Having put so much effort into arranging for daycare, household maintenance and work-related chores, women often seem unable to summon up energy to plan spousal life (or social life within marriage). One respondent concludes:

> Day by day [our domestic planning] works very well. One problem is that we tend to plan work-related arrangements like [daycare] very well, but planning for recreation and free time has not been very well organized – "What do you want to do this weekend?" "I don't know. What do you want to do?" It's funny. You get into a habit, don't you, struggling along.

Yet these women refer to their relationships with spouses and children as the most important ones in their lives. Children, especially, seem to have brought them unparalleled joy and excitement. Most of our respondents expected to delight in childrearing, having anticipated this role since adolescence, most say they enjoy it even more than they expected. Some, of course, have found the experience distasteful, odious, boring, repetitive and singularly unrewarding. One adamantly denied liking anything at all about being a parent. Most, however, viewed parenting as "one of the few things worth doing in life."

Conclusions

Feminizing the bureaucracy (Ferguson, 1984) as well as the home involves asking not how women can fit into current structures, but rather how organizations can change to include women in a more egalitarian fashion.

As interviewers, we find ourselves both sympathetic with these women's dilemmas and dismayed with Canadian society for not recognizing childcare as a public responsibility, the fulfilment of which requires systemic change in the current allocation of work and family responsibilities. We greatly admire the resilience, strength and innovation shown by these women as they juggle their multiple chores, often with good-natured humour. We also understand their seemingly passive acceptance of the institutional sexism reflected in discriminatory policies, since it is often beyond their control.

Mothers see the family as the locus of change. Rather than pushing for societal changes, they urge their husbands to shoulder more domestic and childcare responsibilities. This process is necessary, but should be accompanied by institutional practices that accept individuals' rights to combine work and family. Given that mothers are a permanent part of the labour force, our society must begin to address these issues.

Note

Different studies have found different results both in the nature and division of household labour. Discrepancies in the amount of time men and women spend in domestic and childcare chores reported throughout this book result from differences in measurement techniques used in the various studies cited.

Not in Labor Force
33.6

CHAPTER 3

The Traditional Path:
Full-Time Housewives

In the late 1980s, the role of full-time homemaker appears to be headed for extinction. A generation ago, this role typified adult married women, but today it is becoming more and more of an anomaly. This chapter explores the changes that this role has undergone, examines the current realities of full-time homemaking and considers the implications of the demise of this former norm.

How has the social situation of the full-time housewife changed? Contrary to popular assumption, the homemaker supported by an employed husband is a relatively recent phenomenon in Canadian family life. The popularity of the family in which the mother was homemaker and the father breadwinner peaked in the 1950s. In recent years, such families have declined rapidly both in frequency and in terms of public image.

This chapter begins with a historical overview, and goes on to explore the lives of 30 contemporary full-time housewives. In-depth interviews focus on three basic questions.

First, why are these women full-time housewives? As pressure for women to enter the paid labour force mounts, it is important to explore those factors, both social and personal, that continue to propel some women along this traditional path.

Second, how do they see their lives? Our interviewees describe the costs and benefits, satisfactions and frustrations of the way they now live, and explain the strategies they've devised to manage conflicting demands and expectations.

Their comments reveal the difficulties of economic dependence and social isolation. Yet they also show the considerable pleasure and satisfaction these women derive from their lifestyle, which brings us to the final question: What benefits and joys are women losing with the steady erosion of full-time homemaking? Certainly it would not be desirable, even if it were possible, to turn back the clock. But the experiences of full-time housewives provide a useful critique of the increasing domination of all women's lives by paid employment.

A Historical Perspective

For most of Canadian history, the full-time housewife, tending hearth and home while her husband toiled in the paid labour force, was a rarity. Most men and women lived in rural settings, where they shared many agricultural chores. The man tended to control the family's income, the woman might have her own (very limited) sources of cash income, such as selling poultry, eggs or butter at the market. Men and women worked side by side, and their working conditions and work-loads were approximately equal (Armstrong and Armstrong, 1988). Neighbours and members of a couple's extended family often helped shoulder the burdens of family and farm life. In the late 1800s, 80 percent of Canada's population was rural. It was not until 1931 that more than 50 percent of Canadians were registered as urban dwellers (Statistics Canada, 1984). And as late as 1961, one of the ten most common occupations for women was being a farm labourer (Wilson, 1986:95). It was with the development of industrialization and the emergence of full-scale capitalism in Canada that full-time homemaking emerged as the typical social role for adult women. As the family farm became a less and less viable economic alternative, rural families, along with an increasing number of immigrant families, moved into urban areas. There they hoped to take advantage of the (relatively) well-paid – though erratic – employment opportunities in the new factories. The social upheavals of industrialization, urbanization and mass immigration set the stage for woman's role as full-time housewife. In the urban setting, isolated from most employment opportunities both by social custom and by onerous domestic obligations, married women were more and more contained by the domestic sphere. The married woman dependent on her husband's participation in wage labour became the new social norm.

As women became isolated within the private domain, their productive activities became socially invisible. Housewives were not and are not included in official statistics on the labour force. Their efforts within the household, despite their importance to the daily production and generational reproduction of the labour force, have not been included in calculations of the Gross National Product. Women's activities in the home and their volunteer efforts in the community, since they fail to generate wages, benefits, pensions, or profit, were and are formally characterized as non-work (Marsden, 1981). Officially peripheralized, housewives' social and economic status was and is generally seen to depend on that of their husbands.

By the late 1800s, most married women in urban Canada were full-time housewives and, as such, were excluded from the official labour force. Typically, any paid work in which they did engage prior to marriage (such as domestic service or teaching) ended with marriage (Katz, 1975:273). Well into the twentieth century, employers viewed marriage as a justification for automatic dismissal. In 1895, the Toronto Board of Education ruled that it would not employ a woman who had a husband to support her (Roberts, 1976:31). In 1921, the civil service sharply restricted the employment of married women (Archibald, 1978:16). Understandably, young women often attempted to hide their marital status from their employers until pregnancy forced them to abandon any hope of hanging onto their jobs. Only women who were widows or who had been abandoned by their husbands were excepted from this social rule.

Still, as Canada's industrialization advanced, employment opportunities for women increased. By 1901, slightly more than 15 percent of Canadian women were in the paid labour force (Phillips and Phillips, 1983:35). However, most of these workers were young, unmarried women. In 1941, less than 4 percent of married women worked for pay (Bird, 1970:54). The typical married woman worked at home, without pay, taking care of the often heavy responsibilities of domestic labour and childcare: one married woman in four born between 1922 and 1927 (in contrast to one in 20 young mothers today) had five or more children (Cooke, 1986:5).

In the past few decades, married women have moved *en masse* into the paid labour force. In 1951, 11 percent of married women were employed (Phillips and Phillips, 1983:36). Today, approximately 57 percent of married women are in the paid labour force (Statistics Canada, 1987a:87). Less than a generation ago, the overwhelming majority of married women with children under sixteen stayed at home; today only one-third are full-time housewives (Statistics Canada, 1987a:96-97).

It is in highly urbanized areas of the country, and regions with low levels of unemployment, that the diminution in number of full-time housewives is most pronounced. A 1987 survey found that only about 20 percent of Toronto children have two-parent families in which the father is employed and the mother is a full-time homemaker (Johnson and Abramovitch, 1987). Further, it is estimated that less than 50 percent of children in Canada spend their preschool years at home with their mothers, and that two-thirds of children between six and twelve years old have mothers who work full-time or part-time for pay (Cooke, 1986:16-17). Many social commentators see women who devote their efforts exclusively to home and family as an endangered species (Andre, 1981).

Whether or not the housewife is on the verge of extinction, it is clear that the housewife stage in the lives of many married women is changing fundamentally. Early in this century, many young women were in the paid labour force for several years and then got married and had children. Once married, they were generally shunted out of paid employment by a combination of domestic responsibilities, lack of community support, and unsympathetic employers. Typically, these women did not later return to paid employment. The remainder of their lives was spent in childrearing and domestic work. Some did manage to earn an informal income by such means as taking in boarders or laundry.

Starting in the 1930s, more and more married women returned to paid employment after taking time out during their childbearing years. By 1961, one-third of women between 45 and 54 years old were in the labour force. Since that time, more and more married women have returned to paid employment, after taking shorter and shorter breaks from work for bearing and rearing children (Canadian Congress for Learning Opportunities for Women, 1986:59). Although most women still do interrupt their paid work, primarily for pregnancy and childcare, younger women (25 to 34 years) are somewhat less likely to do so, or may do so for two years or less (Robinson, 1986). Sixty-six percent of first-time mothers intend to return to work before their babies' first birthdays (Hock, Gnezda and McBride, 1984). Sixty percent of previously employed mothers return to paid employment two years after giving birth (Waite, Haggstrom and Kanouse, 1985). Most married mothers of still spend some portion of their adult lives as full-time housewives, but the length of that period has decreased (Martin and Roberts, 1984:128-132).

In brief, the location and duration of the housewife phase in married women's lives has dramatically changed in the last few decades. Whereas married women used to interrupt their family lives and seek paid employment to cover unexpected expenses or periods in which their husbands were unemployed, today they interrupt their paid work obligations to fit in pregnancy and early childcare. As a result, when a statistical profile freezes women's labour force participation patterns, fewer and fewer married women show up outside the paid labour force.

The role and image of the housewife in society have also changed dramatically. At one point, the middle-class housewife was revered as the "angel of the hearth" – the embodiment of purity and morality.

Housewives were accorded so much public respect that they were able to launch a number of effective social purity and public morality campaigns (Matthews, 1987). At the same time, the "working" wife was the subject of scorn for having abandoned her children to the care of others. And her husband was derided for failing to provide for her and to control her. As late as 1970, 80 percent of Canadians felt that a woman should not take a job outside the home if she had young children (Boyd, 1981:182).

Throughout the 1960s, as more women began to enter paid employment, the image of the full-time housewife deteriorated. Increasingly, homemakers were seen as old-fashioned, narrow-minded, boring and unglamorous. "Who wanted to embrace a woman who had baby drool on her shoulder and chocolate fingerprints all over her blouse? 3DOTS When the single girl walked away with female sexuality, then the housewife would indeed have nothing to do but gaze wistfully after her" (Ehrenreich and English, 1978:287). Today, such television shows as *Family Ties, Who's the Boss?*, and *The Cosby Show* inundate viewers with positive images of working mothers who manage well-paying, prestigious careers while maintaining extensive family obligations. Predictably, the role of full-time homemaker has lost not only much of its previous appeal, but also its legitimacy. Only 5 percent of contemporary female teenagers agree that "married women should not work if their husbands are capable of supporting them" (Bibby and Posterski, 1985:164). A recent coast-to-coast telephone survey found that 50 percent of Canadian women between eighteen and 29 years old believe that employed mothers can raise their children as capably as full-time homemakers (Maynard, 1988:85).

In large part, these changes in the public perception of the housewife mirror real changes in the content of her occupation. Families have become smaller, domestic technology has improved, and the need for domestic skills has been reduced by the increasing availability of cleaning and food services and "instant" products. These changes have made the housewife's role more and more restricted and ambiguous (Luxton, 1980; Fox, 1980; Cowan, 1983). In many ways, the modern women's movement grew out of the frustration and contradictions of woman's role as housewife (Friedan, 1963). Today, women's activities in the home, as revealed in our interviews, are still in the midst of change – and still a pivotal issue in women's lives.

Methodology

This chapter is based on in-depth interviews with 30 full-time housewives who live in southern Ontario. The women were contacted through snowball sampling, together with other referrals and informal contacts. Almost all the women interviewed live with permanent male partners and have at least one child under sixteen. Four single mothers were interviewed, since families led by single mothers are becoming increasingly common (Boyd, 1988).

The women in this survey occupy a wide range of socio-economic positions. About one-third may be described as well-to-do. Their husbands are professionals, and they enjoy a more than comfortable income. (Three have the unusual luxury of live-in domestic help.) Another one-third could be described as middle-income. Their husbands hold white-collar jobs and they enjoy a comfortable family income. The final one-third are either working-class or poor. Most of these women's husbands hold blue-collar jobs. One of the women has a partner who is unemployed; four are single mothers whose families are dependent on welfare and other forms of social assistance.

Slightly more than half the respondents have some high school, or a high school diploma. Slightly less than half have some post-secondary education. Most of these attended community college, and a handful completed university. This is fairly typical: in Canada in 1983, 59 percent of women between 25 and 34 years old had some high school, or a high school diploma. Only 14 percent had a university degree (Statistics Canada, 1985).

Our respondents' divorce rate is also more or less typical: only two have ever been divorced. And of adult Canadians in general, only 5 percent have ever divorced and remarried (Burch, 1985:11).

Almost all our respondents are between 28 and 40 years old. Two-thirds have one or two children and one-third have three or more children. Given that the average number of children in a Canadian family is now 1.6 (Boyd, 1988), some of our interview subjects have unusually large families. Two-thirds have preschool children at home, and slightly more than half have toddlers and babies (three years old or younger) at home.

All worked full-time for pay at some point prior to having children. Several continued to do so after having children. But most stopped working for pay the first time they were pregnant. Although several worked in such non-traditional occupations as drafting or accounting, the clear majority (like most Canadian women) worked in traditional female occupations (clerical, retail, teaching, nursing). About one-quarter anticipate taking paid employment in the near future or are at present actively seeking employment. Almost all want paid work at some point in the future – when it becomes more feasible or when they have completed retraining programs. Only one woman has no plans to work for pay again.

In short, our respondents seem very much like other Canadian women. With the exception of family size, the only feature that appears to distinguish them from the majority of other women of their age is the fact they are presently full-time housewives. They are not, however, a homogeneous group. They differ significantly, not only in terms of social class, education, number and ages of children, and work experience, but also in basic life patterns. Some have been out of the labour force for as little as nine months and are planning an immediate re-entry. Others have been full-time homemakers for thirteen years and have only vague plans for returning to work. (About two-thirds have been out of the paid labour force for more than five years.) Some have spent a number of years in challenging, well-paid occupations; the work histories of others are briefer and relatively unrewarding. Although housewives share a common occupational title and a distinctive economic position, they are divided by significant differences (Freudiger, 1983:214), and any tentative generalizations about them must take these differences into account.

Socialization and Ideology
Traditional gender-role socialization appears to be a simple explanation of why women become full-time housewives. Women, it could be argued, opt for full-time homemaking when they have been brought up to expect to be taken care of by their husbands and to devote their energies to home and family. One might presume that growing up in a traditional family – with a stay-at-home mother as a role model and an emphasis on marriage and family as life goals – heightens the probability that women will become full-time housewives.

Specifically, it might be expected that women who become full-time housewives would be likely to come from traditional families (the mother a housewife and the father a paid worker); to plan their lives on the basis of marriage and family; to put little effort into developing skills for paid employment; and to express agreement with a traditional, male-dominant ideology. In other words, full-time homemakers may be thought to have been brought up to be more conservative than other women when it comes to gender-role issues.

In fact, our interviews offer very little support for this notion. First, only half the respondents have mothers who devoted their adult lives to the role of traditional, full-time housewife. The other half have mothers who participated in the paid labour force at some time after their children were born. Some of these women's mothers worked full-time throughout their children's lives, while others took paid employment only after their children entered high school. The notion that our respondents are simply modelling their own behaviour upon their mothers' does not seem very useful. However, several clearly feel that having a mother who went out to work was undesirable. One, who has been a full-time homemaker for five years, has poignant memories of her employed mother:

> I really missed her being there – like coming home to an empty house. And later she'd be busy with her homework. I remember my mother sitting there, marking papers, and I'd have to wait to say I wanted help with *my* homework. I would have liked to have a mother who stayed home and baked and did all those wifely things. I did miss that.

Such negative experiences may help motivate some women to stay home. However, since almost all of our respondents plan to return to work before their children are adult, this is clearly only a small part of the picture. Further, since about half the women who had working mothers have neutral or positive recollections, it does not seem that this particular aspect of their experience was pivotal. One, who has been home for five years, comments, "I don't remember missing her. It just seemed to be the thing that she was supposed to do." Another, who worked part-time for four years and has been home full-time with her three children for a year, recalls a mother who needed to work: "We didn't mind – it brought in extras. We thought it was great, and we saw that she was happy doing it. When she stayed at home full-time, she was not a happy mom."

There is little evidence that these women had unusually traditional aspirations when they were younger. Asked about their dreams when they were eighteen years old, most talk in vague terms about marriage, family and a career or job. Very few dreamed exclusively of marriage and children. But in discussing their plans for careers or jobs, many are noticeably vague about both their long-term and short-term goals. They experience life as something that happens to them. These comments are typical:

> I always knew I would graduate [from university] and get a degree in something. Marriage – I guess I thought that would happen to me.

> I thought I was going to get married and have children – but I was heading towards university and a degree and a good job, and I don't think I ever thought how the two would interact.

The few women who had concrete plans and goals for their paid work-lives stand out in stark contrast.

This pattern of vagueness, confusion and passivity does not differ from that expressed by women who work for pay. Nor is it atypical of young women today. Many young Canadian women are growing up with unrealistic expectations about marriage and family roles, and unclear approaches to their future paid employment. For example, "Girls seemed to be less concerned than boys about advancement or managerial positions. Although they expressed a desire to be rich, they were less likely than boys to feel that they could get this wealth through paid work" (Baker, 1985:160; see also Bibby and Posterski, 1985:162-166). In this respect, the early aspirations of full-time housewives are not unusual.

Early gender socialization does not appear either to slot women into full-time homemaking or to set up significant obstacles to this option. A young woman who is strongly committed to a particular educational program or who has her sights on a specific occupation or career has relatively little flexibility in terms of marriage and family. But an unfocused and vague approach to adult life is compatible with a whole range of possibilities. Life may be "on hold" until the right partner comes along, or until after the children are born. Gender socialization maintains the possibility of family-centred priorities. Other forces determine how women actually sort out the demands of home and work.

Full-time housewives are not right-wing women, as stereotypes suggest they might be. Some research has proposed that women who are committed to paid employment are less influenced by traditional sex-role stereotypes and "are more willing to take an active stance in trying to reach goals" than are full-time homemakers (Stokes and Peyton, 1986:307). But the interviews conducted here do not support such a conclusion. Although a few of the women interviewed are conservative and support a very traditional approach to family life, deferring to their husbands' right to make decisions and affirming the necessity of women staying at home with children, the clear majority rejects this conception of gender roles. For example, asked whether they would recommend that other women stay at home with young children, more than three-quarters say they view this as a very personal decision that depends on life circumstances and interests. They do not feel it is necessary or even desirable for all mothers to stay home and they are expressly not judgmental about women who choose to take paid employment while their children are still young. One, a full-time homemaker for eleven years, speaks for most of her fellow respondents on the question of whether women should stay at home:

Not really. Other women seem to want to be out working – myself, I'm just the opposite, I prefer to be home so that I can get things done, and I don't fall behind, usually. Yeah, I would say if women want to go out and work, they should.

Similarly, on other gender-role issues, most tend to express views no more or less liberal or conservative than those of the full-time and part-time workers discussed in Chapters Two and Four. For example, most indicate that decision-making is shared in their households. All but a few insist that they share difficult decisions. More than three-quarters *disagree* with the notion that "It is better if the man works to support the household and the woman takes care of the home." Few appear to see being a full-time homemaker as a political statement about the role of women in society or in the family. Along with 62 percent of Canadian women, however, the majority do agree that "when there are small children in the home, if possible the mother should not work" (*Chatelaine*, 1988:85). None agree that "Fathers should be the top boss of the family in this country."

If their past socialization has not already done so, it is unlikely that present-day socializing pressures will push women to adopt an unusually conservative viewpoint. More than three-quarters of our respondents associate with full-time homemakers, full-time workers and part-time workers. Few are friends only with other full-time housewives. Similarly, most have female relatives who work full-time or part-time for pay, as well as some who are full-time homemakers. Asked how their peers and extended family would react if they did take paid work, most anticipate a positive or, at worst, a mixed reaction. One, who's been home five years with two preschool children, has a typical response:

I think they would be supportive, if only because it's my decision and they normally would be supportive of my decisions. They know I wouldn't make a hasty decision.

Similarly, most do not see their husbands as holding strong views in favour of or against working mothers. A few say their husbands either feel that women benefit from having careers, or would appreciate additional family income. Several others see their husbands as strongly supportive of women staying home with young children. Most believe that, while their husbands appreciate their presence in the home, they would also support or at least accept any future decision to return to the work force:

Well, he doesn't really say one way or another. I think if I had a job, he wouldn't mind the extra money, but there are a lot of times he says he makes the money and he doesn't mind if I'm not working. The only reason he would like to see me work is if it's going to be to my benefit – if it's something I enjoyed, he would say, "go for it."

It's my decision [to stay home] and he supported me. If I want to get a job then that's fine.

In short, past and present gender socialization and gender-role ideologies do not appear either to account for women becoming housewives, or to prevent them from doing so (see also Greenstein, 1986). In most respects, housewives' socialization and gender attitudes seem to be very much like those of women who work outside the home. Given the increasing public acceptance of working mothers, we need to consider other factors in order to understand why our respondents are presently full-time homemakers.

Economic and Work Considerations
Not surprisingly, many analysts have focused on economic factors to explain the ways in which women balance work and family. It seems reasonable to expect that, all other things being equal, women who live in affluent families are more likely to stay home than women whose families are in need of additional income. In societal terms, women's movement into the paid labour force has been directly associated with increased pressure on family income (Armstrong and Armstrong, 1984:166-178). From 1980 to 1984, the average income of Canadian families (using constant 1984 dollars) fell by $2,180 (Lindsay, 1986:15). It is not surprising that more and more married women have entered the paid labour force to help maintain their families' standard of living. Diverse research indicates that her family's economic resources and needs are important determinants of a woman's participation in the paid labour force (Michelson, 1985:40; Lowe and Krahn, 1985:16).

It is clear, however, from the class variations between the women interviewed here, that family income is an imperfect predictor of whether women become housewives. Women stay home when their family income is in excess of $70,000 – but some stay home when their families live on less than the national average ($35,770 in 1984). And some stay home when their families depend on welfare payments and food banks.

There are several immediate explanations for this lack of connection between family income and women's participation in the labour force. Highly educated women tend to be less likely than others to interrupt their careers for family obligations. Because they have invested heavily in acquiring an education, and because they probably reap greater economic rewards and satisfaction from employment, they are inclined to stay in their jobs or return to work more quickly (Burch, 1985:31; Martin and Roberts, 1984). They are also more likely to marry well-educated men, who earn above-average incomes. As a result, although their family incomes are certainly high enough to allow such wives to stay home, other factors pull them into the labour force. Conversely, women with average or less-than-average education may need additional income, but find that the costs of paid employment (transportation, a larger wardrobe, daycare) outweigh the returns of a low-paying job.

The state of the national or local economy also figures prominently in prompting women to stay home. A housewife may seek employment only to find that none is available in her area. Given the current unemployment rate in certain regions of the country (18 percent in Newfoundland and 10.5 percent in British Columbia as of 1987), lack of work may be a crucial factor (Statistics Canada, 1987a). Further, a woman seeking part-time work, or flexible work-scheduling, may find that such options are unavailable in her occupation or in her community (Martin and Roberts, 1984:125).

Finally, the quality of women's paid work-lives may interfere with the effect of economic and other factors. If a woman is in a challenging, interesting, or pleasurable work situation, she may be less likely to leave work than otherwise, or may do so for shorter periods of time.

Those of our respondents who were in satisfying occupations are relatively enthusiastic about returning to paid employment. Some have enjoyed highly successful careers as teachers, nurses, or executive secretaries, to which they look forward to returning later in life. About one-third were in the paid work force until their late twenties or early thirties, and worked in challenging, well-paid positions. Says a former director of public relations:

> I really did enjoy my job. I thought I would go back part-time for a while. I did freelance for a while – but I soon found I was so preoccupied with the baby, I gladly left [the job].

Other women found their paid employment oppressive and unrewarding, and were happy to leave. Generally, they are not looking forward to returning to the labour force. There is not, however, any clear connection between work satisfaction in a career, as opposed to a job. Some women have fond memories of their work experience as bank tellers and clerks – particularly of friends they met at work. Others had careers in nursing and teaching that they strongly disliked. Most have mixed feelings about their paid employment. They miss some things – getting out, having money, being with adults – and definitely do not miss others – getting out of the house early in the morning, hours spent commuting, unpleasant supervisors. As in other research (Ferree, 1984), there does not appear to be any simple correlation between social class, quality of working life, and the decision to stay at home.

Economic need and past paid-work experience clearly do affect women's presence in the home. However, other factors intersect with economic and work considerations, and may negate them. Among the most important of these is the availability, quality and cost of daycare.

Daycare Issues

As has now been widely documented, there is insufficient quality daycare throughout all of Canada. For example, in 1984, licensed care in centres and family homes furnished 172,000 spaces, but an estimated two million children needed daycare. The problem is particularly pressing for very young children (seventeen months or less). It is estimated that 133,000 spaces are needed for this group, but only 11,622 are available (Cooke, 1986:51-52). Since the overwhelming majority (80 percent) of children currently in care are in unlicensed settings, there are many concerns about the quality of care. Finally, the costs may be prohibitive. *The Cooke Report on Childcare* found that a couple with an average income and two children – an infant and a three-year old – would pay between 14 and 21 percent of its combined income for daycare. Since a wife working full-time is, on average, contributing less than 40 percent of the family income, it is clear that daycare expenses erode the economic benefits of mothers' work (1986:12-15).

Daycare is an important issue to about half the women interviewed here. Several indicate that the lack of daycare is a major impediment to their paid employment. One, who has been home for three years, says:

> When I was first pregnant and I started taking my seventeen-week [paid maternity leave], I had decided to return [to work]. What changed my mind primarily was talking to the public health nurse who came around after the birth of my son. I was talking to her about daycare. I hadn't really looked into it. I had assumed it was always there – only to be told that she takes her child to a home [private, unlicensed] daycare, that there aren't too many to be found and that the quality was rather poor. So I started doing some digging on my own, talking to people, phoning places, and I found out. I was astounded by the lack of quality, the mediocrity of the whole daycare system, the poor pay of the childcare workers. The whole situation astounded me and at that point I said, there's no way I'm going to take my son into a situation like that.

Since her husband works irregular shifts in addition to holding a part-time job, she has not been able to manage a part-time job.

Another woman, who has been a full-time homemaker for eleven years, worked for a short stint while her children were very young and found the costs prohibitive:

> I was working to pay them, not for myself. I would work 40 hours a week and then maybe I got 20 hours' pay after I paid the sitter and stuff.

Other research confirms that many homemakers would look for work if satisfactory childcare arrangements were available, and that women whose daycare does not work out end up at home (Floge, 1985:153).

The availability of daycare is not, however, a universal concern. The remaining half of our interviewees have never explored daycare possibilities because they decided early on in their marriages to stay home with their children for some time. They typically comment, "I never really looked into it." However, it is also clear from their comments that their negative impressions of the daycare situation reinforce their decision to stay at home. Daycare is seen as "not as personal," or "not as caring" as care in the home. Daycare centres are seen as places that are understaffed and where kids "pick up every bug there is." So we see again that the scarcity of attractive childcare alternatives contributes to the likelihood that women will opt for time out from paid employment.

Family Pressures and Supports

Household work-loads vary considerably depending on such factors as the number and ages of a woman's children (Schafer and Keith, 1984). Presumably, one of the important pressures to work full-time as a housewife is the presence of heavy family responsibilities and / or the absence of assistance.

It is not surprising that most of our respondents interrupted their paid employment when they had, or were about to have, very small children at home. At this stage, the care, feeding and supervision of children is particularly time-consuming. More than half of the interviewees still have at least one child under three years of age at home. Women with young children report spending about ten hours a day in caring for them, and talk about the strain of the unrelenting tasks. Since "little children are so demanding," mothers feel that they "spend every hour" they're awake monitoring their children's activities. Older children are not necessarily more independent. Several interviewees have children who are handicapped or frequently ill. Further, as previously mentioned, one-third of the respondents have more children than the average Canadian family.

In addition to childcare responsibilities, there are the everyday household chores – food shopping and preparation, housecleaning, laundry, organizing – which must fit into the day. According to their own calculations, most of the women devote 30 hours or more to household tasks (excluding childcare). Other research suggests that a young mother with two preschool children is devoting 38 hours a week to housework and 70 hours to childcare, and is thus "on call" 98 hours a week (Kome, 1982:49).

Predictably, most of our respondents are busy from early morning till late evening. Most receive little assistance in managing their heavy domestic burdens. About one-third talk specifically about the time pressures of their husbands' jobs, which result in the husbands' prolonged absences from home (see Finch, 1983). Men who juggle multiple jobs, or who travel in their work, spend little time at home. Women end up shouldering "90 percent of the responsibility." One, married to a corporate executive, says:

> My husband spends so much time away from home. He doesn't contribute that much to taking care of our son. So it's just not practical [for me to work]. He doesn't do much, but I don't expect him to do any more, because he's run quite ragged at work.

Another, whose husband works as a crew member on a Great Lakes tanker, says:

> He's not home most times. So I'm the only one here. But when he's home, I like to have him help.

However, even husbands who are more available contribute relatively little time to household and childcare tasks (see Luxton, 1983; Bernardo, Shehan and Leslie, 1987). Asked about the division of chores in their households, almost all our respondents indicate that they handle most of the routine responsibilities. According to these women's reports, only a handful of men devote ten hours or more per week to sharing this work, and most contribute an average of three hours a week:

> Before the child was born, we divided [tasks] more equally. Then his job got more demanding and I stopped working, so it was just natural that I would do more. There's getting to be less and less participation [on his part]. I'm hoping there will come a time when he's not quite as involved in his work, and gets more involved in childrearing.

Other research corroborates this pattern. Michelson, for example, found that full-time housewives in Toronto spend seven times as many hours on housework and childcare as do their husbands (while mothers who work full-time for pay spend three times as many hours as their husbands do on such duties) (1985:65).

Similarly, children, even those who are more than eight years old, provide little real assistance in the house. Though almost all children are expected to make some contribution to keeping the household clean and orderly, their tasks are generally nominal – "cleaning up toys, making their own beds, helping with cooking." Their mothers estimate that they contribute one or two hours per week to the performance of household chores.

The sheer weight of all the chores and responsibilities these women manage may make paid employment impossible at this point in their lives. One, who plans to return to work when her baby is a little older, describes the difficulties she anticipates:

> You get home when it's dark. You have maybe two or three hours left to do something you want to do. You have two days every week to bundle all the things you want to do into. How can people do it? I admire women who can handle it. They have to get up earlier, do more, race off to work without thinking about the kids too much. It must be awful. I admire women who can do it and stay sane and not have nervous breakdowns.

It is not only the volume of domestic tasks, but also the nature of such tasks, that pull women into the home. Most of our respondents feel that they are the most qualified, reliable and committed providers of care for their children – particularly preschool children, who are seen to need almost constant adult supervision and stimulation. The women talk often of the importance of "being there" for their children:

> [If I worked full-time] I'd worry about if something happened to the kids and I wasn't able to be reached. I'd worry about being able to keep up the house, provide good meals – home-made meals – whether I'd be coming home every night with the bags from Burger King or McDonald's. [I'd worry about] being there for their problems.

Available substitutes for childcare by the mother are seen as significantly inferior and / or inadequate. Strangers are not seen to care enough about the children, or to be reliable. Given their paid employment responsibilities, husbands are not considered serious alternatives.

Care by the women's mothers, and, to a lesser degree, mothers-in-law, is seen as the best option, but is often unavailable. Ultimately, if the job is going to be done, and done well, these mothers see themselves as the best candidates – at least while the children are young, the domestic tasks onerous and the family's economic need not too pressing.

In sum, various pressures push and pull at women with young children. A range of powerful societal forces have encouraged the increased participation of mothers in the paid labour force. These include the decline in real family income; the increased availability of education and employment for women; the de-skilling of domestic labour; the growing public acceptance of working mothers; and women's increased control over how many children they will have, and when. Other pressures encourage women to spend at least some time as full-time housewives. These include inadequate daycare alternatives; periods of intense domestic obligation; traditional gender socialization; the time demands of husbands' employment; high rates of unemployment among women; the restricted nature of women's paid employment alternatives; and the reluctance of husbands to share equally in domestic and childcare responsibilities. The interplay of such factors in individual women's lives is complex, subtle and dynamic. Economic pressures and school-age children do not necessarily result in women's paid employment, just as economic ease and preschool children do not inevitably produce full-time housewives. Conditions change, sometimes dramatically, over time. A local daycare centre opens, or a part-time job becomes available, and the balance of pushes and pulls may be dramatically altered.

In broad historical terms, it appears that the general trend is towards stronger and stronger pushes into the paid labour force and less and less time out at home. For women presently working as full-time homemakers, the pressure to stay at home still outweighs any immediate draws into paid employment. For most, also, the benefits of being at home – at least temporarily – balance any perceived problems.

Drawbacks of Being a Housewife

Although most of our respondents are committed to their current role, they are not oblivious to its limitations. The work is often boring, repetitious and unrewarding. A clean house, a home-cooked meal and a made bed are almost immediately undone. Asked to describe their most satisfying household task, most are hard-pressed to come up with an enthusiastic response. Generally, they select non-routine tasks such as gardening, sewing or entertaining. Day-to-day housework is enjoyable in terms of its product (a clean room or house) but not in terms of its process. One woman, asked how much satisfaction she gets from housework, replies:

Very little. I like a clean house, a tidy house. Immediately after I've done it I feel satisfied, but then the next day it's dirty again. I don't enjoy it.

Another laughs, and says:

Seriously, I get a lot of satisfaction from it. It's just wonderful to watch a really grungy floor come clean under my fingertips. No, really, I don't mind housework. Mind you, I wouldn't get a job as a cleaning lady.

A third says, "I don't like doing it [housework], but it's got to be done."

The fragmented nature of the work exacerbates the problem. Efforts to get the kids dressed and off to school are combined with and interrupted by plans for supper and the preparation of school lunches. Often the demands of childcare are in complete contradiction to other domestic duties. Clean floors are in irreconcilable opposition to active children. Domestic work does not flow unimpeded along one clear, continuous channel, or produce obvious end products.

Not only is the work itself often tedious and difficult, it is generally done in isolation from other adults. As more and more women return to the paid labour force, housewives' contacts with other adults become severely limited:

When I first decided to stay home my son was under a year. I felt lonely and I would get depressed at times, because I wouldn't have the companionship. I could never arrange very easily to go out with my friends. I could talk to them on the phone, but my son was a demanding child. I'd get on the phone and five minutes later, he was pulling on me. [It was] really just the loneliness, the lack of companionship with my friends.

Echoing the results of almost two decades of research, these women find much of their work unsatisfying and frustrating (Oakley, 1974; Luxton, 1980).

Women's domestic work-loads tend to increase once they stop working outside the home. Most of our respondents indicate that their husbands' contributions to domestic labour and childcare have decreased since they became full-time housewives. One, who has three young children, typifies the pattern:

When I was working full-time, I laid down the law. If we're both bringing income in, then we're both going to share the jobs around the house. Some of those [decisions] have carried over. [However,] since I've quit work, he has slacked off.

Michelson's Toronto study generated similar results. Husbands of housewives contribute less time to household activities than husbands of employed wives (1985:66-67). On average, full-time housewives spend more time (seven hours a day) on housework than married women with paid jobs (four hours a day) (1985:44-45; see also Blumstein and Schwartz, 1983:144-146).

If unchecked, the work-load seems to expand endlessly. Several women comment on the tendency of childcare and household responsibilities to absorb all the time in a day. They caution other women to make sure they preserve some time for themselves, for their own interests and activities. One, who has been a full-time homemaker for twelve years, finds that her husband, children and even neighbours are inclined to take advantage of her perceived availability for chores and errands. Her comments reflect a recurring theme:

> I think, as much as you try to avoid it, you fall into doing too much for your family. Plus other people tend to know that you're available for certain things. They know you have more free time to do things. I think the biggest thing [is that] you have to be careful with your own family – you might fall into doing too much for them, husbands included.

The housewife's work generates scant social reward, and no economic gain. The old stereotypes – "do you work or are you a housewife?" – persist. Most of our respondents indicate that they are aware that housework is not prestigious (see Eichler, 1977; Bose, 1980). For some, their husbands' lack of involvement in household tasks and, particularly, in childcare, underscores the lack of recognition given to their efforts. Several speak defensively about not spending their days idly – "eating chocolates and watching television." One, a well-paid professional who left her career in her early thirties, reflects this concern:

> The longer [you] stay at home, the more difficult it will be to get the confidence you need to go out and look for a good job. And also, when people ask you what you do, you wish you could tell them you were a brain surgeon.

Another, home with three young children, says, "It's just nice to see someone writing a book on stay-at-home moms – bringing us out of the closet and the shame that we stay home." Ironically, being a full-time housewife has taken on much of the stigma once associated with working mothers.

These women's concerns about their public selves are related to fears of becoming boring. They worry that they will fall into the stereotypical role of "the boring housewife," whose conversation revolves around "what the dog did today":

> You get out of the mainstream. I can understand so easily why marriages fall apart. I'm terrified of becoming boring to my husband. Right now he's fascinated at having a child. I think it's important to get out [of the house]. Sometimes I feel that I'm talking baby-talk all day.

As long as wives are engaged in a full-time occupation that is not socially valued and is largely foreign to their husbands, these are serious concerns. Research suggests that when marital partners are living very different lives with dissimilar concerns, they may experience difficulty communicating and sharing. When partners share both paid employment and housework (role homophily) marital solidarity appears to be stronger (Simpson and England, 1983).

In light of this lack of social validation of their day-to-day activities, it is not surprising that full-time homemakers are found by researchers to be more anxious and more unhappy than wives who are employed (Coleman and Antonucci, 1985; D'Arcy and Siddique, 1985). One recent study concludes that "employment outside the home is associated with improved mental health among married women" (Kessler and McRae, 1982).

The lack of social reward is reflected in and reinforced by the lack of economic return. The value of housework in Canada in 1981 was between $121 billion and $139 billion (Swinamer, 1986:42). Yet housewives receive no wages or salaries. In the early 1970s, members of the women's movement launched a campaign for wages for housework (*The Activist*, 1975), urging the state to recognize housewives' important contribution to society by paying them for the many services they render. Today, women's groups continue to press for wages for housework and pensions for homemakers (Woodsworth *et al.*, 1987). These campaigns have enjoyed little success.

Generally, full-time housewives are economically dependent on their husbands. Very few of our respondents have such under-the-table sources of small income as babysitting or housecleaning. Most are not concerned about their economic dependence on their husbands. Some feel guilty about leaving the wage-earning to their husbands, and others are uncomfortable about not having money of their own:

I have to rely on my husband's money. You don't feel quite as free to spend it when it's not your money. I don't feel I can just go shopping for me unless he says it's okay.

[If I had my own money] if I saw something I wanted, I wouldn't have to ask my husband. I don't ordinarily have to ask him anyways, but it would give me a sense of accomplishment.

[Being a housewife] seems to be frowned upon by a certain section of people and I feel, without the pay, I have less worth.

Most, however, are not worried about long-term ramifications. They assume they could easily re-enter the labour force if anything happened to their husbands or their husbands' jobs.

Nevertheless, the optimism of this particular group of women should not obscure the real problems of housewives' economic dependence. More and more Canadian marriages are ending in divorce (McKie, Prentice and Reed, 1983). Recent calculations suggest that about one in three will do so. Many divorces produce families headed by single mothers. In 1981, one of every ten children in Canada was living in such a family. Employed mothers, who earn approximately 68 percent of what men earn, and contribute on average only 30 percent of the family income, are often ill-prepared to provide sufficient economic support to their families. Fifty-six percent of families led by single mothers live in poverty (National Council on Welfare, 1988:2). Women who are full-time housewives, whose paid work has been interrupted and whose job skills may be outdated are particularly vulnerable to impoverishment.

Staying married, however, is sometimes equally unsatisfactory. As discussed in Chapter Two, recent research on violence in the family suggests that women who are not employed outside the home are more vulnerable than others to serious abuse by their husbands. It is economic, rather than psychological, dependency that traps women in "severely abusive marriages" (Kalmuss and Straus, 1982). MacLeod found that 80 percent of the women in Canadian shelters for abused women were not employed outside the home (1987:20). Women are more likely to stay in abusive situations when they fear that they and their children will live in poverty if they leave. Given the high rates of wife abuse in Canada, the problem of violence is a serious consideration.

Even housewives with enduring, peaceful marriages may encounter difficulties. Inevitably their domestic and childcare responsibilities lessen as their children grow. Today, only about seven years elapse between the birth of a woman's first child and her last (Michelson, 1985:35). The last child of a 50-year-old woman who has between two and five children will typically leave home when the mother is about 52 years old (Burch, 1985:25). Women can expect to live to about 79 years of age (Statistics Canada, 1984a:2). The continued reduction of their domestic responsibilities while they are still in the prime of life and face many more productive years may result in "the empty nest syndrome." In contrast to women in most other societies, Canadian women today cannot anticipate "that the traditional mother's role [will increase] in complexity and importance as she grows older" (Greer, 1984:23). One woman, home with a six-month-old baby, talks about her mother's unhappiness at being left with no real purpose in life:

> My mother was your traditional housewife. Now she's 53. In the last ten years, the children have left her and she has had absolutely nothing to do. She has fallen into a severe depression. She was just left with nothing to do, and I'm really afraid of that. For years and years, she devoted herself completely to her family.

With few social and no economic rewards, with no signposts marking advancement and accomplishment, and with the steady elimination of household responsibilities, it may be difficult to derive satisfaction and meaning from a life devoted to homemaking. It is not surprising, then, that almost all the women interviewed here plan to return to paid employment. In the interval, personal and societal pressures to stay at home outweigh both countervailing forces and potential drawbacks. Furthermore, most of our respondents see the benefits and pleasures of this domestic interlude as greater than any difficulties or long-term penalties.

Benefits of Being a Housewife

Most of these women feel that their decision to stay home was the right – in fact, the only – choice, for both themselves and their families. A few are eager to return immediately to full-time paid employment, and most are occasionally frustrated or angered by the burden of housework or the lack of appreciation from husbands or children. But almost all feel that their presence at home is, for now, necessary and desirable.

In particular, they point to their maternal responsibilities and pleasures, and to the leisurely pace of life they experience relative to that of employed mothers. Having more control of their time allows them to both fulfil and enjoy their parenting role.

Repeatedly, they speak of the importance of "being there" for their children. Clearly, their conception of what parents do gives much weight to being available *whenever* the children need attention:

I've helped them along; I'm the one who's been there to do it. I get a good feeling knowing that they have the freedom to come to Mommy if they need something. They're not going to somebody else with their needs.

As I grew up, I knew that my mom was there. I felt very secure and I felt there was a lot of love there. I felt a lot better coming home to a mother than just coming home to an empty home. I think that is important to children.

"Being there" encompasses a complex range of feelings and attitudes. As previously mentioned, our society differs from many others in that there is generally no other relative who can help mothers shoulder the responsibility of childcare (Greer, 1984:22). Thus part of being a good parent is simply being physically present for one's children. Mothers who work for wages often express guilt about not satisfying this requirement. They seek to assuage their guilt through routine phone contact or "quality time" spent with children.

The importance of "being there" is often explained in terms of the ability to respond to an emergency or crisis, whether minor or major. Our respondents fear that, if they were employed, they would not be able to provide "the compassion that a woman needs to give her kids on an emergency basis." They worry about what would happen if "something happened to the kids and I wasn't able to be reached." These concerns may seem somewhat unrealistic, since even full-time housewives are not always home or always accessible. But these women derive relief and peace of mind from knowing they are there for their children. Furthermore, they avoid situations in which their maternal responsibilities might be challenged or contradicted by their obligations as paid workers:

When you have a full-time paid job then I think your responsibility is to that job. If you have a family at home, that could become a problem. You're pulled one way or the other and you don't know exactly what you want.

When I was working in Toronto, I was running an office but I was also trying to run a home. And your kids are in daycare, which doesn't always work. If they're sick, you've got to miss work or your husband has to miss work, which can be stressful. The pressure of keeping it up is too large, really.

"Being there" permits mothers a complete involvement with their children. They have the time to monitor, direct and control their children's upbringing (see also O'Donnell, 1985:89-90). The children become more fully the "product" of the women's labours, right down to the smallest details (Mitchell, 1966:109):

> I want to be there in the morning, make sure they're dressed properly. I want them dressed the way I want. The way their hair is combed – just trivial things like that. That's just me.

> I get great satisfaction with every step they learn because I've taught them.

> She is going to be taught to be a good, polite person. That's really important to me. I feel that children who are in daycare or are being looked after by babysitters aren't learning anything about simple discipline or morals.

Inevitably, even the best parenting – providing the children with both "wings" and "roots" – is not a life-long career. The day-to-day routine of providing attention, discipline and direction is often difficult and stressful (Genevie and Margolies, 1987:15-53). However, while it lasts, it is clear that motherhood provides most of these women, much of the time, with a tremendous sense of personal satisfaction and fulfilment from "the most important job that I've had to do."

Finally, being with their children also provides substantial day-to-day pleasure. Aside from the satisfaction of fulfilling responsibilities and the pride of producing "good" children, there is the fun of sharing children's discoveries and joys:

> I get a tremendous amount of satisfaction. I enjoy it immensely.

> [My satisfaction is] immense, immeasurable. I think it's grand – watching minds open up – the questions they ask, being there to answer them.

> One hundred percent satisfaction; wonderful; tremendous to see how he has developed from a seven-day old colicky baby till now. Watching him grow and become a person, expressing his own thoughts.

> I love it. It's totally satisfying, and you get tenfold back.

Not surprisingly, our respondents are not unequivocal. There are times when they feel "totally fed up," times when they feel "a little bit of sadness" as the children grow independent, and times when the children simply "drive you nuts." Overall, however, it is clear that these women's relationships with their children are important sources of pleasure and joy. Simply witnessing their children's development is one of the most interesting and enjoyable dimensions of their lives. "If mothers can stay home with their children, they should, because there are so many things that are fun to see, that are interesting to see." For many women, paid work experiences hold little such fun or interest (Armstrong and Armstrong, 1983).

Further, knowing that they occupy a distinct and central position in their children's affections provides these mothers with an important feeling of worth and fulfilment. In adult life, in which there is often little recognition or reward for work inside or outside of the home, being the centre of a small child's universe may be intensely gratifying. "I know there is a lot of love there returned and it makes me feel good." In a society that seems increasingly characterized by impermanence and replaceability, these powerful emotions may be deeply rewarding and satisfying.

However, as several feminist analysts have pointed out, a lifelong commitment to full-time mothering may enmesh women "in a potentially destructive web of dependency, responsibility and isolation from the public sphere" (Levine, 1983:37). Women who have lived their lives for and through their children and husbands have found that their sacrifices were neither appreciated nor desired. As Helen Levine points out, "Motherhood, like fatherhood, is no substitute for a life's work, an adult way of being in the world. It is potentially a caring, intimate and responsible relationship – no more, no less. Making motherhood the central job for women has rendered it destructive to mothers and children" (1983:33). Full-time housewives who devote their adult lives to mothering their children may find as they approach middle age that the rewards and recognition they have received are insufficient.

However, almost all our respondents feel that they have more free time, or leisure time, than do mothers who work for pay:

> If I had a paid job, I can see that I'd have far less time for my son, my husband, myself. Just because there are so many things that have to be done.

Not surprisingly, a wide variety of research corroborates this impression. Michelson, for example, found that full-time housewives spend more time in sleep, personal activity, socializing and passive leisure than do their husbands, whereas wives who work full-time for pay have 40 minutes less leisure time per day than do their husbands (1985:66-67).

Employed mothers have less time for their children and less time to sleep than do those who are not employed. Even though mothers with full-time paid jobs reduce the time they devote to housework, they spend more time in obligatory tasks (housework, paid work, childcare) than do full-time housewives. Non-employed, married mothers have 66 minutes more free time every weekday than do employed, married mothers (1985:44). Thus, full-time housewives avoid the role overload that plagues employed mothers.

Many of the women interviewed here left the paid labour force in search of this more relaxed and freer pace of life. They now speak appreciatively of having more flexibility and better control of their time:

> If I decide to sit down and have a cup of coffee on my own I can do it, I have that choice, I have that time.

Although this free time is often quickly filled with obligations, these women feel that they have more discretion than do employed mothers in dictating the pace and content of their work:

> I find more to do when I'm at home. I seem to never be able to keep up with the housework. I'm probably a better housewife than I ever was – I've been scrubbing baseboards now. But I don't have to do it. I can sit and read.

> You find things to fill up your time. So I don't really have more *free* time [but I do have] more *choice* in how I use [my time].

Greater flexibility, choice and control result in a relatively relaxed and orderly life. There is time to manage and organize domestic and childcare activities. Life is not a constant rush. Mothers' assumption of full-time responsibility for running the household and organizing everybody's time produces an ease in family life. The household work and childcare are done at a reasonable pace during the course of the day, not left till the evening or morning, and not always intruding on leisure or recreation. When comparing their daily lives with those of women who work full-time, or to periods when they themselves worked full-time, our respondents emphasize that they have the time to "enjoy what [they] have" – their houses, children and husbands. Staying home removes "a lot of pressure."

These women have time to devote to themselves. Almost all participate in activities outside the home. About three-quarters are involved in at least one volunteer activity, such as church groups, Brownies, charity work, or the PTA. Such work is important and satisfying to many:

I can sneak some free time. For the most part I am out doing volunteer work and doing my things. I have a little more choice [than employed mothers] of *where* I put my leisure time.

I get a great deal of satisfaction from [volunteering] and I feel I'm contributing something to the things I'm involved in. I'm giving, but I'm getting more out.

About two-thirds of our respondents are involved in some form of education – ranging from piano lessons to university courses in Japanese. Within this group, about half are not working towards any specific educational goal and are taking courses simply out of interest or to develop a hobby. The other half have specific goals, such as obtaining licences or degrees in order to re-direct their occupational lives:

I just feel this is the time I should make a decision about what I do later.

I've got to get through school and do what I set out to do.

I want to make a career change. Retail is not that conducive to family life. I think I'd like to do something in the organization field.

In short, these women derive important benefits from the time they spend as full-time homemakers. There is considerable satisfaction and enjoyment in "being there" for the children and the household. In light of the nature of most paid work alternatives, there may be considerably more pleasure and fulfilment to be found at home than in the workplace. In particular, there is often greater control over scheduling, and greater opportunity to set aside personal time.

The Decline of the Housewife: Gain or Loss?

It appears that fewer and fewer women will become full-time housewives, and those who follow this path will do so for shorter and shorter periods of time. Already, full-time homemaking has been reduced from a life-long occupation to an interruption, brief or prolonged, in women's participation in the labour force. Barring any major changes in the economic and social order, married women will continue their move into paid employment.

Many other Western countries are also experiencing this trend. In the United States between 1950 and 1980, there was a 108.8 percent increase in the rate of participation in the labour force of women with children six to seventeen years old, and a 263 percent increase in that of women with children under six years old (Gerson, 1985:233). In Great Britain, the employment rate of women whose youngest child was between eleven and fifteen years old increased from 60 percent in 1969 to 78 percent in 1979 (Martin and Roberts, 1984:120-121). And Sweden, which has provided extensive daycare along with extended parental leave, now has the highest percentage among Western nations of employed mothers of children under seven years of age: 85 percent. Not surprisingly, "being a full-time housewife in Sweden today carries a stigma" (Popenoe, 1987:180).

There are clearly strong reasons to view this trend as a victory for women. Women, even if they are married and have young children, are now free to work in the paid labour force. No longer do rigid institutional rules and social mores restrict women's lives to the domestic sphere, or enforce wives' dependence upon their husbands' wages. This victory won, however, we still need to evaluate the costs and benefits of full-time homemaking for women.

In many respects, the lives of the women interviewed here corroborate the critique of full-time housework emanating from the women's movement in the 1960s. The women complain of the unending and heavy burden of domestic labour. They complain of isolation and lack of social recognition. Full-time housewives are still penalized in terms of economic dependence, job or career opportunities and social prestige. To the degree that women are forced into full-time homemaking – by any combination of gender socialization, heavy domestic and childcare responsibilities, inadequate daycare, lack of social supports and lack of opportunities and rewards in their paid employment – the erosion of this way of life is an advance for women.

However, as we have seen, this is not the whole story. Our respondents feel that they enjoy considerable advantages in staying home. The pace of their lives is more orderly and relaxed. They have time for themselves and time to enjoy their children, their husbands and their personal interests. For some, this is an opportunity to reassess and perhaps reorient their employment lives. Life is more manageable; it isn't always rushed. To some degree, being a full-time housewife is a critique of the frantic pace and role overload experienced by the employed mother – and a demand for more time, more control over time, and more pleasure.

Although becoming a full-time housewife may be unpalatable and / or impossible for most women today, it is possible to construct social alternatives that take seriously the needs expressed by women who take this route. For example, workplaces could adopt flexible employment policies that would be compatible with the fluctuating demands of people's domestic and personal lives (Luxton, 1987). The 40-hour-week is not ordained, any more than the 48- or 60-hour-week. Women (and men) with very young children need work arrangements consistent with their family lives, such as job-sharing and part-time work schedules. Increasing the availability of paid and unpaid extended leave would allow workers to respond to family and personal needs. Quality daycare – either in the workplace or in the community – would allow both women and men to better integrate paid employment and parenting, and would give parents greater peace of mind.

What should be possible, with the development of enlightened social policies, is the integration of paid employment with many of the benefits of full-time homemaking. As modern feminists recognize, the goal is not to eradicate alternatives for women, but rather to elaborate and improve existing options. If the role of full-time homemaking in women's lives and traditions is indeed going to be obliterated, it is important to listen to the voices of housewives, and to work to minimize women's costs and losses and maximize their benefits and gains. Social policies should extend the range of women's possibilities by helping to sustain some of the pleasures of homemaking, while increasing women's access to high-quality, reasonably paid employment.

Conclusions

Once the full-time housewife is placed in her social and historical context, several conclusions become apparent.

First, the notion that full-time homemaking should constitute adult women's life-work is a relatively recent and short-lived historical phenomenon. From the early 1920s to the early 1960s, it was commonly accepted that, upon marriage, the average woman would retreat forever from paid employment and devote herself to her home and family.

Since the 1960s, full-time homemaking has become a phase of shorter and shorter duration in most mothers' lives. Economic, social and personal pressures currently impel women into paid employment for more and more of their adult lives.

Second, there are important variations between full-time housewives. In particular, the duration of the housewife phase varies considerably. Some of our respondents plan to spend less than a year as full-time housewives. Others have already devoted several years to full-time homemaking and have unclear, long-term plans to return to the labour force. Respondents' past work experiences and levels of education appear to help determine how long they will be housewives. However, as previously stated, any generalizations about housewives must be prefaced with an acknowledgement of housewives' diversity.

Third, women become full-time housewives as a result of a complex interplay of social, economic and personal factors. Many considerations intersect to push or pull women into or out of paid employment – including whether the family can get by without a second income; how heavy the domestic responsibilities are; whether there are attractive childcare alternatives; how women conceptualize their maternal responsibilities; whether husbands support their wives' paid employment; and whether manageable, attractive paid work is available. Which factors predominate depends on the individual woman's life circumstances (such as the presence of a new-born infant, a disabled child, or a helpful mother-in-law), the community or region in which she lives (which determines her employment opportunities and the availability of daycare) and such social and economic pressures as rates of inflation and unemployment.

Fourth, since all women are affected by external social and economic factors, the values and attitudes expressed by our interview subjects (particularly regarding gender roles) inevitably resemble those of women who work for pay. Few of our respondents could be characterized as right-wing women. Being a housewife does not seem to be rooted in a commitment to traditional, patriarchal conceptions of woman's role and of family life.

Finally, the realities of housewives' day-to-day lives are rife with contradictions. Our respondents' descriptions of their daily routines clearly support much of the 1960s' feminist critique of housework as tedious, isolated and unrewarded. However, these women seek, and generally find, compensations for these drawbacks. In particular, the challenges and satisfactions of motherhood, together with freedom from the strictures of paid employment, are felt to compensate – at least in the short term – for the negative attributes of being a full-time housewife.

These women's accounts attest to their efforts to construct meaningful and manageable lives while being buffeted by powerful social, economic and familial forces. Most acknowledge their low social status and lack of economic independence, as well as the dire implications of divorce and family violence, the potential for long-term occupational penalties and the tedium of household tasks. But for many, there are few other options. The possibility of positive change or positive action seems remote. Their choices have been made for them by the conditions prevalent in our society, including lack of good daycare, lack of flexible work-scheduling, and limited possibilities for paid work. With no attractive alternatives in sight, it is not surprising that most of our respondents prefer to stress the benefits of full-time homemaking. At least, as they say, they are there for the children.

Part-time
18.3

CHAPTER 4

Balancing Responsibilities:
The Part-Time Option

Part-time work is often presented as a desirable and necessary option for women.[1] It is seen as allowing the flexibility required in the domestic sphere, as well as the personal satisfactions and independence derived from paid work. Women who work part-time often feel that they have "the best of both worlds."

Underlying this view are certain assumptions about women's roles and life situations: the benefits of part-time work are primarily depicted in light of women's responsibilities in mothering and homemaking. Part-time work is expected to relieve women of their isolation in the home and provide "extra" income for family purchases, while not to interfering with household demands. The part-time worker is presented as free to shop, prepare meals, taxi children to after-school activities, and keep her home clean. Thus the part-time paid work of mothers is discussed mainly in the context of family life.

In the voluntaristic – or free-market – view, women complacently enter part-time work because it is compatible with their domestic role. Employers may not expect high levels of commitment from women who work part-time, since they often conclude that these women are working only temporarily. Further, they may not be concerned about such workers' job satisfaction, assuming that they find their satisfaction in the domestic domain (Weeks, 1980). Critics suggest that this position ignores the constraints put upon paid work options by the unavailability of full-time work (or other work arrangements), the lack of adequate daycare policies and facilities, other limitations stemming from the structural organization of society, and the family situations of individual women (Lowe and Krahn, 1985; Smith, 1983; Wilson, 1986).

The voluntaristic position is based on four assumptions: that in considering their paid work options women are faced with a choice, that they choose part-time work because of their maternal ideology and commitment to domestic responsibilities, that women (and especially mothers) may be less committed to paid work than men, and that mothers' part-time income merely supplements the family wage. This stereotypical view of women as secondary earners and men as breadwinners may be used to justify low wages, a dearth of benefits, and lack of job security for part-time workers. Some employers see part-time work as a service they offer, since it allows women to maintain the skills and business contacts that will help them return to work once their childcare responsibilities are diminished.

The conventional assumption that workers predominantly choose part-time work to suit their own needs (Wallace, 1983) is not borne out by statistics on involuntary part-time work. More than one-quarter of all the people, including 26.3 percent of all female part-timers, who worked part-time in 1987 did so because they could not find full-time work (Statistics Canada, 1987). In that year, 71 percent of unwilling part-timers were women; 72 percent of those women were between 25 and 54 years old, and 84 percent of them were married (derived from Statistics Canada, 1987). Between 1975 and 1986, full-time employment grew by 15.2 percent and voluntary part-time employment increased by 41 percent – but involuntary part-time work rose by 375.4 percent (Akyeampong, 1986:144). The highest rates of involuntary part-time employment are in community, business, and personal services, where women between 25 and 54 years old (and young people between fifteen and 24 years old) are concentrated (Levesque, 1987; Akyeampong, 1987). Insufficient opportunities for full-time work force many married women of childbearing age into part-time work.

The overall growth in part-time work between 1975 and 1986 may be primarily due to trends within industries – particularly in community, business, and personal services (Levesque, 1987). Similar trends are apparent in Britain, where the dramatic increase in married women's employment is largely attributable to the expansion of the service sector in post-war decades and the concentration of women in part-time jobs in this sector (Yeandle, 1984:7-8). These growing industries have traditionally drawn on women's labour. In contrast, the manufacturing sector – which has traditionally drawn on men's labour – has a low rate of part-time employment, and its share of total employment decreased between 1975 and 1986. In short, part-time employment opportunities are rarely available in the most coveted job categories (Levesque, 1987).

Despite its clear significance, it is only in the last few years that a substantial body of research on part-time work, and specifically on part-time women workers, has been developed. The information available includes surprisingly little input from part-time women workers themselves. With the exception of a few studies, such as those by Michelson (1985), Kervin (1983), and Beechey and Perkins (1987), research and policy have been based largely on mass statistical data, rather than on part-timers' actual experiences. This chapter draws on interviews with typical part-time women workers – married women with dependent children – to explore the role of part-time work in women's lives. It should, of course, be noted that the term "part-time work," when applied to mothers of young children, is a misnomer. They work part-time for pay and full-time in domestic labour. They are likely to work much more than people who are not mothers and have a traditional, 40-hour ("full-time") work-week.

Methodology
The data presented here were gathered from in-depth interviews with 50 part-time women workers.[2] Each interview lasted between one and two hours, and included a detailed work history as well as discussion of relations with co-workers and management, relations with full-time workers, attitudes to full-time work, job satisfaction, dreams and aspirations, family relations, division of domestic labour, and background information. Though fairly structured, the interviews allowed ample opportunity to explore issues of particular relevance to each respondent.

As a group, the 50 women interviewed reflect the principal demographic and personal characteristics of part-time women workers (Wallace, 1983). Most are married; only two have been divorced and now live in common-law relationships, and one has recently been widowed. Their average age is 36; none is less than 25 or more than 50 years old; most are between 29 and 43 years old. Most have at least one child twelve years old or younger. Slightly more than half have at least one preschooler, and about one-quarter have at least one teenager living at home.

In this study, "part-time work" was defined, in part, by the self-definition of the respondents. That is, they presented themselves as part-time workers, presumably reflecting their employers' categorization of their jobs. Excluded from this study are unofficial part-timers, such as women who offer daycare in their homes, and seasonal workers, such as women working in agriculture.

Those interviewed work in a broad spectrum of traditional part-time occupations for women. Typically, they are waitresses, teachers, bank tellers, nurses, office workers, social workers, or store clerks. In fact, all but one (who teaches part-time in a university) work in either sales, service, or health. Only a few work mainly with men. Approximately two-thirds work in non-professional jobs (as sales clerks, technicians, or secretaries) and the rest are professionals: teachers, nurses, or social workers. About one-third have some high school or a high school diploma, one-third have some education beyond high school, and one-third have university degrees. As a group, these women are slightly better educated than the typical part-time worker more than 25 years old (1983:47), and better educated than the average Canadian woman fifteen years of age or older (Statistics Canada, 1985:36). This may be a function of the fact that the sample is urban, located in Ontario, and excludes older women. Predictably, then, an atypically high number of these women work as professionals or as managers. Nevertheless, most of our respondents' jobs, like most women's jobs, do not fall into these categories.

Although comparable Canada-wide data are sketchy, the women interviewed, as a group, seem fairly typical in terms of number of hours worked per week and of job tenure. They work between eight and 35 hours per week, with an average of 21 hours. *The Labour Force Survey* (Statistics Canada, 1987) reports an average work-week of about sixteen hours for women part-timers more than 25 years old. The number of hours varies according to the status of the part-timer. One of our respondents works exclusively on an "on call" basis. Most are permanent employees, and rely on long-term hourly patterns. Several are contract, or temporary, workers. Most work days; some work nights or shifts. Others combine day work, night work and shift work. Most work on weekdays, but almost one-third work some part of the weekend as well. They have been at their current jobs between six months and fourteen years, with an average of 3.5 years. About one-third have worked one year or less. Wallace reports that women part-timers 25 years old and older usually keep their jobs for one to five years (1983:62).

Rates of multiple job holding and levels of unionization among these respondents also conform to national statistics. Only two of the women currently hold more than one part-time job, although several have held more than one job simultaneously in the past. According to Wallace (1983:65) less than 3 percent of all part-timers (men and women of all ages) are multiple job holders.

Only eight of our respondents are union members. In 1984, 18.8 percent of part-timers were unionized, including 13.6 percent of male part-timers and 20.9 percent of female part-time workers. In contrast, 40.9 percent of (non-agricultural) full-time workers, including 44.2 percent of men and 35.2 percent of women, were in unions in that year (Coates, 1988:51).

Almost all our respondents identify themselves as willing part-timers. Adult women part-timers typically do not indicate that they have been forced to accept part-time work because of the absence of full-time work. According to a recent *Labour Force Survey* (Statistics Canada, 1987), 33 percent of all part-timers (of both sexes and all ages) are willing part-timers. Women constitute the vast majority (85 percent) of this group. More than twice as many women (39 percent) as men (17 percent) indicate that they work part-time simply because they did not want full-time work. Another 12 percent cite personal or family responsibilities as their main reason for working part-time. Significantly, more than two-thirds of women part-timers between 25 and 54 years old – and almost three-quarters of married women part-timers – give one of these two reasons for their part-time work.

How do mothers assess their own decisions to work part-time? Did they follow the part-time work option in light of motherhood and domestic duty? Or were they forced into part-time work by a lack of full-time paid work opportunities, the inadequacy of childcare policies and facilities, and their own financial constraints? The interview data offer a glimpse of the complexities mothers encounter in balancing the conflicting demands of their various roles and responsibilities in the face of current economic and political realities.

Work and Life Plans: Courses of Uncertainty

For many married women with children, part-time work presents itself as an acceptable arrangement that allows time for domestic responsibilities, childcare, and personal needs. What stands out most in a review of our interviews is these women's contentment with their current situations and with life's possibilities.[3]

Most do not see their current part-time jobs as part of a general or long-range plan. Their aspirations seem, on the whole, to be very similar to those of the full-time paid workers and housewives discussed in Chapters Two and Three. Almost half indicate that, when they were eighteen, they thought that they would marry and that their husbands would provide for their financial support. Although these women realized early in their lives that they would spend periods of time in the labour force, they usually had contingency plans for their occupational futures, rather than distinct courses of action. Most clearly did not regard paid work as requiring elaborate planning early in life.

At some point in their lives, nearly all these women have worked in various full- and part-time jobs. All have worked full-time for pay, and most expect to return to full-time paid work at some point in the future. Most gave up their full-time jobs when they first gave birth and subsequently spent some time as full-time mothers and housewives. The length of this period was between four months and 16.5 years. The average time spent exclusively in the home was 4.5 years, and half the women stayed home less than two years. Most enjoyed this time; only a few describe it in predominantly negative terms.

With regard to planning their lives, the women interviewed may be divided into three groups: waiters, dreamers and planners. Overwhelmingly, these women's plans were vague. Most describe themselves as moving from job to job or wandering through a particular job until life's circumstances – marriage, childbirth, relocation – necessitated a change. Very few mapped out a specific career path, followed it, and expect to continue with it.

The waiters are currently developing plans that often include major occupational changes. They have made few career plans until now. Many have experience in various types of paid work, but do not wish to continue with any one of these when they return to full-time paid work. At this point, most are studying their options, and are not quite prepared to commit themselves to a particular line of work. Many are considering upgrading their education or developing new skills. They are becoming anxious about their amorphous future. They have wandered in and out of paid work for a number of years, sometimes taking uninteresting or otherwise undesirable jobs. They have accepted this uncertain course because of their family obligations, but now they want to chart more definite paths for themselves.

Many of those who had no concrete career goals prior to marrying and having children describe part-time work as a natural and reasonable course of action for women. Most agree that being a mother conflicts with having a career. One, who has recently obtained a Master of Library Science degree and works part-time as a librarian, explains:

> It's a difficult thing to suggest to someone [to work part-time],
> because many people who work full-time are in a very different
> situation than me. Because I didn't establish myself in a career
> and then have a child, so I didn't have to make a decision about
> giving up a job for a child. I didn't have a job to give up, so it was
> much easier than having to decide, "This is all I want to do, work
> part-time."

This woman, like many of our respondents, suggests that it is suitable for women to develop career plans once their children reach a certain level of independence. In this way, job options may be selected to accommodate family life and children's needs. This is presented as more logical than committing oneself to a career and then adapting one's family to its demands. Some of these women are still hesitant to make specific plans, since they cannot necessarily anticipate what will happen in their families. Others worry about losing control over family matters. Yet all are adamant about having "time to develop careers" or "time for [themselves]" in the future. Some are beginning to take steps towards specific goals.

The dreamers, too, moved into their current positions with little planning and remain uncommitted to any particular direction. Unlike the waiters, they are not yet ready to develop alternative courses of action. One explains her career path as the least offensive option open to her when she moved with her husband to the United States after he enrolled in a professional school there. Others describe their position as a choice by default: they happened to be "at the right place at the right time," or they simply "stumbled" into a job.

The dreamers are often anxious about the future, and are unsure about what they would eventually like to do. They see the future mainly in terms of what they don't want, certain only that they do not wish to pursue further opportunities in their present line of work.

Finally, a minority of our respondents are planners. They are usually, but not exclusively, professionals who developed clear goals early in life. They often express interest in moving up a career ladder, and are emphatic about the importance of planning for participation in the labour force. Yet not all are satisfied with their current positions. Some are disappointed with the limited challenge posed by their jobs and the lack of variety of work available to them. Others relate their dissatisfaction to their part-time status. The professionals (nurses, teachers, social workers) often entered these careers due to the perceived flexibility of such work, as well as its compatibility with domestic and maternal obligations. Those in non-professional jobs (retail sales, daycare, clerical work) see their work as appropriate to the fact that their primary emphasis is on family life. They have invested fewer years and resources in developing their skills, and are generally pleased with the way they can move in and out of the paid labour force to accommodate their maternal and domestic responsibilities. They assume that job opportunities, and especially opportunities for part-time work, are quite widely available – so that if they "quit today," they can "always get another job tomorrow."

None of our respondents is greatly concerned about the labour market losses or career set-backs that may result from spending a number of years in part-time work. Missed career opportunities and part-time work are simply regarded as personal costs paid for the rewards of family life. A 29-year-old social worker with two children is emphatic about her priorities:

> At this time, going up the ladder in my profession is not a priority. My family takes precedence over my career, as long as I have something to keep me busy, keep me stimulated.

In most cases, even the planners do not view their current jobs as part of their long-term plans, but rather accept them as unplanned, or at least temporary, but necessary activities.

Part-Time Work and The Domestic Sphere: Balancing Demands

What is most striking about the women interviewed is their expression of contentment with their present circumstances. Although they often see themselves as having to juggle too many roles at once, they seem to be satisfied with their own circumstances, given the alternatives of full-time paid or unpaid labour.

In light of this expression of contentment, four general themes emerge from our interviews. First, working part-time allows women to accommodate their families' needs in their schedules. Part-time women workers have a manageable mix of paid work and unpaid family obligations.

Second, their part-time work provides most of these women with a sense of personal satisfaction. It grants them a degree of independence and gives them a sense of privacy – of having "something of their own," not shared by family members. Still, they spend most of their time caring for their families and managing their households.

Third, working part-time provides these women with some opportunity to reorganize the division of domestic labour in their homes, and to establish family support for the idea of their working for pay. Many regard this as a coping strategy both for now and for the future, when they expect to undertake full-time paid employment.

Finally, part-time jobs – as opposed to the full-time paid or unpaid alternatives – provide women with a sense of accomplishment in striking a balance between home and workplace.

Accommodating Family Priorities and Needs

Our respondents typically mix references to their part-time work with allusions to family life and domestic obligations. All say that they work part-time primarily due to family responsibilities and pressures. The preference for part-time work expressed in this group is more pronounced than that reported in a recent survey conducted for the 1986 Task Force on Childcare, in which 31 percent of mothers in two-parent families, and 35 percent of single parents, regarded part-time work as the option most suitable to their own and their families' needs (Cooke, 1986:11).

Asked why they are working part-time and whether they would recommend part-time work to other mothers, almost all emphasize motherhood:

> Number one, to be home with my baby. That's about it; if I
> didn't have any kids, I'd work full-time.

Women working part-time are believed to be substantially compelled by their domestic and maternal obligations, and in this way are often perceived as similar to full-time homemakers (Eagly and Steffen, 1986). Some of our respondents express strong feelings of guilt and concern about the time they spend away from home while working part-time. Even when their children approach adolescence and become quite self-sufficient, these mothers worry about being absent from their families. For example, one 43-year-old teaching assistant, whose sons are teenagers, says she has "a lot of interest in the family" and feels that "even working part-time has limited my life in the home."

Not only do these women describe their part-time work primarily in relation to family responsibilities, but they often picked the particular jobs they did "because they fit in with the family." They frequently praise their jobs, or sympathetic supervisors, for accommodating their families' needs. Some schedule their hours to coincide with the school day. Others prefer evening work, so that they will not inconvenience family members. One woman explains:

> I felt that my priority was the children and I'd stay home with
> the children and try to work my career around that, and that's
> why I predominantly work in the evenings – so my children's
> schedule is not disrupted that much.

Part-time jobs and tailored work schedules allow these women to protect and separate their family roles from the encroachment of their other obligations. Asked to describe their work routines, most begin with their domestic responsibilities. The part-time job is often characterized as inconsequential – a distraction from the main event.

Given these views, it is not surprising that many espouse a traditional conception of woman's role in the family. For example, almost half agree that when there are small children at home, the mother should, if possible, not work for pay. (As discussed in previous chapters, this is a majority position among Canadian women.) One woman explains:

> Children need a mother and most fathers are always out of the
> home. Especially, children today really need the guiding hand
> of a mother at home as much as possible. The male, I think,
> should still be the one that goes out into the world and earns the
> bread. And the woman, if she has children at home, should be
> guiding her children, looking after them, educating them in real

values, true values – not leaving it to teachers or to the rest of society. The preservation of the family has always been number one on my list, and I've sacrificed for it.

A 41-year-old teacher with three children explains her position on this issue:

> I wouldn't recommend part-time work if you have to work when your children are at home. If you can get part-time work when your children are at school or daycare, fine. But it's really important that you have that traditional time with them, and unfortunately not everyone can do that.

These women are convinced that their mothering could not be adequately replaced by the work of babysitters, daycare workers, or anyone else. They and their husbands are concerned about their children's future, and refuse to "take a chance" by not being there when they're needed. Most of these women do not condemn others who work full-time and are away from their children a great deal of the time. Such arrangements are simply not suitable to them, since, in the long run, they may not be in the best interests of family life.

Only a few of our respondents indicate that they would switch to full-time paid work if it were possible to hire household help. Presumably, for most, their domestic role is central to their feelings of self-worth. Many are not interested in hiring outside help under any circumstances. Significantly, most of the professionals and non-professionals alike identify their families as the most satisfying aspect of their lives. The exceptions refer to such things as getting a degree, personal growth activities, religion, and "life itself."

A noteworthy minority stresses other important factors in the decision to work part-time. Several women are working part-time so that they may continue contributing to the economic support of their families while attending school. One waitress / bartender refers to her part-time job as allowing her the financial independence to go to school. Others emphasize miscellaneous factors, such as the opportunity to have time to themselves, or time to relax.

Some have opted for part-time work after they – and their families – experienced the stress of combining domestic labour and full-time employment. A 42-year-old kindergarten teacher explains:

> I tried it one year when my sons both went to school. My husband was trying a business venture. I thought, "Okay, I'm going back." It was too much. I was awfully tired. To me, it was too demanding. I thought life was too short.

This attitude is reiterated by most of our respondents, sometimes quite bluntly:

> What will I be doing five years from now? Working full-time. [Ten years from now] I'll be dead from working full-time.

Although most intend to work full-time in the future, they are well aware of the strains this will produce.

For some, a part-time work schedule is a strategy for avoiding the dilemma of choosing between family and workplace in times of crisis. A 36-year-old nurse who has two young children explains:

> There's a lot of pressure on the family [if you're] working full-time and looking after things. Even though it brings more money in, there's a lot of stress – getting the kids out to school, or getting them dressed and up to the babysitter. Children could be sick. And trying to decide who's going to stay home with the child, especially if the woman is career-minded – who's going to look after the children? Neither one wants to stay home, and it's a lot of pressure I don't need and I don't think anybody needs, especially when the children are young. It's best that one works part-time and the other works full-time.

Working only part-time for pay is a means of avoiding conflict. One woman describes part-time work as her strategy for maintaining a happy marriage:

> I'm really afraid to work full-time, because the jobs I have always had have been incredibly demanding – by my choice – and the energy that I had afterwards was to do something totally different, to go out and party, to go to the movies. I look at working full-time and I say, "What am I going to be like by eight o'clock?" My husband works incredibly hard and gets home very often between seven and eight. So what happens when we both hit that front door at eight o'clock, both with really demanding jobs? What happens first of all to us? And what happens, of course, to the children? But I'm first of all concerned about us, because I think the children will manage one way or another, but I'm not sure that he would. He needs a traditional wife that's still fun, so it wouldn't work.

Her rationale for working part-time as a store clerk – a job that she describes as embarrassing – indicates how much this woman has internalized the responsibility for domestic labour, family security and happiness, and romantic love. Most of our respondents do not question such accommodation.

In brief, most of the women interviewed here suggest that they work part-time because of their obligations within the traditional, patriarchal family. However, this is only a part of their motivation. Woven throughout their comments is the view that part-time work allows them to satisfy personal needs and is preferable to full-time work, either in the home or in the paid labour force. As Yeandle (1984:158) found in Britain, part-time work is the employment strategy women adopt – along with other measures, such as engaging husbands in domestic work and paying for childcare – "as a means of organizing their lives to undertake paid work and carry out the tasks of domestic labour."

Satisfying Personal Needs

These women do not define their part-time work simply or exclusively as an extension of their work as mothers and homemakers. Rather, they see it as a means of achieving personal goals (such as completing their education) and rewards (such as a degree of financial independence). In their references to family responsibilities and maternal ideology, three themes recur: personal fulfilment, growth and autonomy; economic self-worth and independence; and personal enjoyment in work and in domestic relations.

Two-thirds of our respondents refer to part-time work as an avenue to more satisfying and fulfilling personal lives. Several are convinced that they learn more than when they were full-time housewives. Part-time work provides structure:

> I think a lot of women need it. They need that kind of push to get out. If it's a voluntary thing, you won't do it. So I would recommend it as a kind of fulfilling thing.

Significantly, about one-third emphasize that working part-time allows them to grow as autonomous individuals. They work not only "for the sake of the family," but also for themselves:

> Part-time work is one thing that's totally yours. There's an ownership to part-time work. The experience is really yours; [it doesn't belong to] anybody's mother, anybody's wife.

Most recommend that mothers should work part-time in order to achieve some independence:

> I feel every woman should do something for herself – have that little bit of independence, get away from the kids. Because you can get into a rut.

A degree of independence also functions as a safeguard against the anguish and isolation of domestic life. This 34-year-old loans clerk is completely committed to being a mother, but regards her part-time work as a "safety valve":

> I think the family is very important. I don't think any small children should be left unattended over a long period of time. So I think in order to take care of your children, take care of your house, and get out and have an outlet outside of the house, one should work part-time. Because if you stay all day with the kids – I've seen where the tendency is to start to go a little nutso.

Many of our respondents have entered part-time work not for the satisfactions derived from the work itself, but rather in a cloud of negativity, wanting to avoid the boredom and stagnation of full-time domestic labour. Most are reluctant to complain about the periods they spent at home in domestic labour – since they believe these periods were essential to fulfilling their maternal responsibilities – yet many point out what they have gained since having re-entered the work force. One, who spent six years in full-time unpaid domestic labour, relates her feelings of entrapment in that situation:

> It's what I felt was right, but I felt trapped. I felt really dependent on my husband. I was delighted to be home with my daughter – that was everything I thought it would be. But on a really personal level – for me, not me as a mother – I was pretty freaked out by it.

Thus part-time work is seen as an opportunity to have a sense of existing, and possibly growing, "outside the family." The economic pay-off, of course, makes feelings of self-worth and self-sufficiency concrete. About three-fifths of these women refer to the economic significance of their employment. One-third talk specifically about the reward of feeling productive. Most must work in order to make the family budget balance. Only about one-quarter say their families could get along without their income. They relish the sense of accomplishment from contributing to their families' economic well-being, and many emphasize the degree of personal freedom they gain by earning their own income.

These women see part-time work as instrumental in allowing them to enjoy both their jobs and their families. A part-time waitress describes her job as leaving her enough time and energy to maintain a sense of control over family matters, "to keep up with things like parent-teacher night, Brownie night – the odd thing that comes up." In particular, a part-time work schedule frees time for personal growth and special interests, while leaving enough time for family relations:

I'm interested in a lot of areas. I don't want to be locked into something and have to sacrifice some other area, so with part-time [work] I can juggle things. So if something comes up, my family has the priority. It's very important. It gives me that flexibility.

As this 49-year-old clerical worker indicates, the demands of a household, a family, and a full-time paid job may leave too little time for spontaneity, unscheduled events and the development of new interests.

Many respondents refer to being "free," having "free time" or "time for myself," and being able to "control my own time." Most are presently engaged in extracurricular activities. Many volunteer in the community, some are in physical fitness or personal growth courses, and about one-third are enrolled in educational courses. Part-time workers tend to be involved in volunteer activities in the community: 21.2 percent of part-timers – but only 15.6 percent of full-timers – do volunteer work (Statistics Canada, 1985).

In particular, many respondents mention having enough time not only to care for their children, but to enjoy them as well. A 33-year-old clerk with three children elaborates:

If you work full-time [and have] small children at home, you're cheating yourself, missing a lot of the good things about having children. I found when I was working full-time, [having] small children became more of a burden than a pleasure.

Another woman feels that working part-time gives her "more time to do more things with my children and enjoy my children more." Most of our respondents simply want to be able to accompany their children on school excursions, or to sit and watch an episode of *Sesame Street* with them, without worrying about schedules.

Other domestic duties are also more gratifying when time pressure is lessened. Says a store clerk with two children:

I don't want the kind of pressure that builds up inside so that you resent doing these things. There's a certain amount of pleasure to be derived from doing household chores, satisfaction from having done it – it looks nice, you feel good – but you don't feel any of that if you're really angry that you have to do it and you don't have the time.

Finally, it is clear that, for many of these women, working part-time obviates much of the guilt attached to working outside the home, and thus allows them to enjoy their paid work.

Most of our respondents look forward to the days on which they work; several have ambivalent feelings about these days; only a few simply look forward to getting them over with. Of course, any reference to or measurement of satisfaction found in life and in work must take into account the terms in which a situation is assessed. These women generally prefer part-time work because – *at this point in their lives,* economic need, domestic responsibilities and personal considerations make the alternatives unsatisfactory.

Establishing Domestic Support

Most of our respondents indicate that even part-time work requires a redistribution and / or reassessment of domestic tasks. A 35-year-old university professor explains:

> A lot depends on who your mate is and how amenable they are to your working and how willing they are to participate at home. I suppose that's one of the things that women should consider when they're thinking about part-time jobs – whether they're still going to be stuck with everything at home plus working outside, or whether they're actually going to get some relief at home.

Research has concluded that mothers who work part-time for pay are more exploited than most other workers, since their part-time paid jobs are usually taken in addition to their full-time responsibilities at home (Sharpe, 1984:188).

For more than half of our respondents, moving into part-time paid work (from full-time homemaking) has required a perceptible change in the division of domestic labour. Other respondents may fail to recall such a change because they have been working part-time for many years, or because such factors as a husband's unemployment have obscured the change. Our interview data support White's (1983:23) argument that some women may use part-time work to alleviate the inequality of their domestic situations. Presser (1986) found that most women working part-time rely on their husbands to provide childcare, and that part-time workers are more likely than others to be constrained in their work-hours due to inadequate daycare options. In some industries, a "twilight" (early evening) shift was especially created so that working mothers could schedule their part-time work for times when their husbands were home, in order to avoid babysitting fees (Sharpe, 1984:51).

Usually, women's part-time jobs require that husbands, and in some cases children, assume a greater share of domestic tasks. Our respondents have often had to train their husbands in the art of household management and in the subtleties of childcare. One, who refers to herself as a "deli girl," explains:

> I said to my husband and my daughters in the fall, when I started working, "I need everybody's help. I can't just do this by myself." He's had to take responsibility for the kids for those two entire evenings – remind them if they have homework, and get them to do it.

Most respondents indicate that their domestic burdens have been eased by increased contributions from family members. One, a house cleaner, remarks: "I'm lucky. When I'm out cleaning [other people's] houses, my husband cleans my house." About one-third state that their spouses have taken complete responsibility for at least one domestic task traditionally accorded to women, such as doing the dishes, making the evening meal, vacuuming, doing the laundry, or ironing. All but a few feel that their spouses do their fair share, or more than their fair share, at home. Almost all the mothers of children at least eight years old indicate that their children (especially the girls) make important contributions to domestic labour by preparing meals, washing dishes, or tidying up.

Many of our respondents comment that their own attitudes towards domestic labour have had to change. A 41-year-old teacher with three children describes the difficulty she faces in changing her family's and her own attitudes:

> Your family assumes that when you are around, you're going to do that job. Your husband assumes it, you assume it, and your children assume it, and it takes a long time to change that assumption. I assume the kids aren't capable of cooking a meal, and yet they are. I have to change my own thinking as well.

Many have had to learn to accept that "if the house is messy and everyone is busy, then the house will simply have to stay messy." Others recognize that they need to put aside the notion that things must be done "a certain way," to ask for and to accept children's and husbands' help, and to relax their own standards. Some of our respondents reflect further on the changing sources of their satisfaction in work and in life. A 39-year-old secretary elaborates:

> When I was much younger, I did feel that a woman's place was in the home, cooking good dinners, tending to the garden, or

creating a warm household – although I feel somewhat different now.

Such changes in attitude reflect society's questioning of traditional attitudes and values. But they are contingent on personal experiences and ambitions.

Some women force changes in their domestic arrangements when they realize that they are experiencing work satisfaction only vicariously, through their husbands. One, who hopes to pursue a career in art but has worked as a store clerk for seven years, says:

> Initially, I felt that his ambitions were important enough for me that I was willing to do junk in order to facilitate him doing the good stuff. Now that I have my own stuff I want to do, to some extent he's started doing more. But he doesn't really care about it in the same way I do.

These women have generally decided to work part-time when their domestic tasks have become sufficiently manageable to make this possible. They anticipated that working part-time would alter the division of domestic labour in their families. But most see their husbands as "helping" them with duties that are primarily their own.

If we establish a continuum of domestic relations, with a completely one-sided arrangement at one end and an egalitarian arrangement at the other, most of the women interviewed fall into a middle position – what Luxton (1983) refers to as the "separate spheres and co-operative relations" category.[4] Most of the respondents do not insist "that their paid work must never interfere with their ability to care for their husband and children or to run their households"; "that domestic labour is entirely women's responsibility"; or that it is inappropriate to "expect their husbands to help" (1983:31). Although they support "the idea of changing the division of labour and in practice . . . are instituting such changes by exerting increasing pressure on their husbands and children to redistribute both the responsibility for, and the carrying out of, domestic labour," they do not seem committed to a completely egalitarian model of domestic labour and they do not in general agree that "regardless of necessity, women with young children have the right to paid employment if they want it" (1983:33). Part-time work is a compromise that reforms, but does not revolutionize, traditional domestic relations.[5]

Our respondents see part-time work, not as a capitulation to the traditional, limited role of women in the family, but as an improvement on that role, an expression of personal autonomy and growth, and an explicit rejection of the overload entailed in working full-time both for pay and at home.

Striking a Balance

Although heavily influenced by their childcare responsibilities, mothers who decide to work part-time also consider such factors as their own personal satisfaction, both at home and at work. Our respondents repeatedly refer to "getting something out of everything," "having a balance," "balancing [their] lives," and "a good balance":

> I would recommend [part-time work] to people who need both of those aspects – mothering, but also the need for some job fulfilment. Basically, it's been good to have that balance.

> I work part-time because I want the best of both worlds. Financially, I don't have to work full-time. I like to balance the time between personal and professional growth, and to spend time with my children.

In this ongoing balancing process, women seek many of the benefits of both working and being at home, while avoiding or minimizing the drawbacks of full-time participation in either sphere. In particular, they are constructing and maintaining a domestic support system (primarily in terms of domestic labour) that facilitates their participation in the labour force, while finding ways to cope with the numerous dissatisfactions that derive from their jobs, their ghettoization in traditional female occupations, and their marginalization as part-time workers.

Seeking balance in their lives through participation in part-time work is often part of these women's pattern of compartmentalizing the various stages of life. For most, the middle years are to be primarily dedicated to the family. One woman explains:

> I figure I'm just setting this time away and then I'll have my time again. I didn't get married until I was 27, so I figured I've had my time for fun and career and it's now time for family. And as I get older, I'll go back to a career, because this is just a stage in my life.

Thus part-time work is seen as temporary. And many mothers, though they recognize its drawbacks and may not like it, see part-time work as an obvious course of action in their particular circumstances:

> I don't know if I want my daughter to be a part-time worker all her life. Because I feel hopefully she won't get married as

quickly as I did, and she'll have a chance to set down some real deep roots in an area of satisfaction. I would not recommend it to her unless she did get married and have children.

How Does Part-Time Work Rate?

Our respondents generally feel that the way women balance their desires and duties is a private affair. With few exceptions, each of these women views part-time work as her personal decision, based on her own family situation – including her family's income, the number and ages of her children and her status within the labour market. Although these women are generally aware that most mothers face difficult decisions, they see such difficulties as private troubles, rather than public issues (Connelly and Christiansen-Ruffman, 1987). A few are politically engaged in promoting women's issues through their unions or in their communities. Yet even they are structurally constrained in terms of available alternatives, and view their accommodation of their families' needs in personal terms (Luxton, 1987:173).

Literature on part-time work often emphasizes such disadvantages as low pay, scarcity of benefits and opportunities for advancement, lack of job security, and lack of on-the-job training (White, 1983; Wallace, 1983; Weeks, 1980; Smith, 1983; Armstrong, 1984; Jones and Long, 1979; Long and Jones, 1980, 1981). Although our respondents discuss these problems and clearly see them as important, what they emphasize is the acceptability of working part-time.

In general, three major themes are apparent in the interviews: that part-time work is a poorly paid and compensated labour category; that, despite its problems, paid work may be a source of mainly extrinsic, but also intrinsic, satisfactions; and that part-time work, for all its drawbacks, is a strategy for maintaining a balanced life situation.

A cursory reading of these interviews confirms the dominant view that married women enter part-time work voluntarily. However, while very few of our respondents emphatically describe themselves as unwilling part-timers, several express reservations about working part-time. Others are vague about their current situations, but will definitely accept full-time work as soon as the "right job comes along." Furthermore, to divide part-time workers into the categories "willing" and "unwilling" vastly oversimplifies people's circumstances. For employers, women in the home and mothers of young children constitute a source of marginal, inexpensive, expendable labour. Yet women are attracted to part-time work by the promise of flexible work schedules and of attention to family concerns (Weeks, 1980). The expansion of part-time work, and its prevalence within the service sector reflects the fact that, although more and more women have entered the paid labour force over the past few decades, they have not expanded their power (Sharpe, 1984:50).

Our respondents' apparent acquiescence to part-time work must not be construed as satisfaction with either their jobs or their general circumstances. They simply view part-time work as the most preferable of their limited options. Their comments on the work itself clearly support previous research findings that the part-time work force is a poorly paid and compensated, marginal labour reserve (Smith, 1983; White, 1983; Wallace, 1983; Weeks, 1980). Although they frequently say they are satisfied with aspects of their present jobs, they juxtapose these assertions with indications of discontent. Most of their problems fall into one of three categories: unsatisfactory pay and / or benefits; differential treatment from full-time workers resulting in feelings of exclusion and powerlessness; and heavy work-loads. In addition, many have specific complaints about their particular jobs.

Respondents were asked to rate their satisfaction, or lack of satisfaction, with various aspects of their jobs. Overall, they rated about one-third of the job components listed as less than satisfactory, and of these, 80 percent were judged to be somewhat or completely unsatisfactory. The women's responses clearly reveal that, while part-time workers may be satisfied with such extrinsic aspects of their work as relations with co-workers and hours that fit their needs, many are dissatisfied with such intrinsic aspects as intellectual challenge, variety of tasks, decision-making responsibility and pay. These results are particularly striking in light of the fact that workers generally tend to express job satisfaction much more frequently than job dissatisfaction. As Archibald (1978:125) notes: "People ... don't like to think of themselves as deserving only dissatisfying work, and this ... probably biases job satisfaction upward" (see also Rinehart, 1984).

Several of our respondents describe their positions as marginal, but beneficial to employers. A secondary school teacher describes the situation in which she and her colleagues find themselves:

> The Board of Education treats us like second-class citizens. It pays us because it has to pay us, but it won't negotiate with us, it won't do anything that looks at our qualifications. We're not given any seniority. If they're going to do hiring, they'll hire the supply teachers last.

Others speak of isolation on the job. They complain that they are seldom included in their workplaces' information networks:

> In terms of staff meetings, I will often be excluded because they don't want to pay me for that extra time. So I'm getting what's

happening from various sources, not necessarily all at once or as clearly as I might. Policies often [seem] confused because I'm not getting them directly. It's frustrating.

With no connections to sources of information, these women are concerned about their ability to do their jobs adequately and about their relations with other employees. They dislike feeling like "second-class citizens" or "a piece of furniture." They want to be treated as individuals, "who [have] some ideas or thoughts." They want to be on the "inside track."

Some are upset with the way management and co-workers treat them. One, a 40-year-old receptionist, resents her supervisor's view of her job "as a privilege, a great privilege that I work four hours a day." Others, when they feel resentment from their co-workers, find it difficult to determine whether this is a result of their part-time status or of other factors.

Almost all our respondents are aware of the dramatic growth in the part-time labour force over the last decade. Several speak of the benefits of part-time labour to employers. One points to part-timers' flexibility and productivity:

> They're worked hard and paid less. Employers get a lot for their money from the part-time person because of the ability to change around days, the extra hours – if you stay half an hour here and there, you're not really going to count it [as overtime].

Another explains how employers gain from part-timers' marginal status:

> They're harder to organize, they tend to be hired on a contractual basis; they have less security, which gives the employer more flexibility in terms of letting people go and hiring people just according to their own business needs, as opposed to feeling responsible for their employees and taking some responsible action.

Part-timers, largely unorganized and unsupported by workplace policies and union agreements, are the workers most vulnerable to employers' whims. Moreover, the low rate of unionization among part-timers represents substantial savings to employers. Non-union female part-timers earn only 57 percent as much as unionized women in part-time work (Miller, 1988:28).

Statements about job satisfaction are difficult to assess – workers can only describe their feelings about their jobs with respect to the alternatives as they perceive them. And for most, especially those in working-class positions, the alternatives are largely unappealing (Rinehart, 1984). Women part-timers in predominantly female job ghettos – with high rates of turnover, few social and intrinsic rewards, and few opportunities for promotion and challenge – may see their jobs as among the best available to them (Moore, 1985). Also, the nature of their satisfactions and dissatisfactions may change over time. One government administrative employee recounts her objections to a newly adopted managerial technique:

> There's been a new merit-rating process instituted. We perceived this as union-busting. It's just put such a wedge in at work. I cannot breathe without telling someone what I'm doing, where I'm going, why I'm going there, when I'll be back. I cannot get up from my desk without being monitored. I can't go to the can: they want to know when I go to the can, when I come back from the can.

In addition, changes in personal circumstances may affect job satisfaction:

> Back then, I accepted it, going out, waitressing, looking after my family. Now my family is older. I work at the same type of job, but I'm not satisfied.

Most of these women, wanting to accommodate their families, accept the dissatisfactions of their jobs, and, in fact, rarely discuss them. As Ferree (1976:439) notes, part-time work is the "preferred compromise" to full-time alternatives.

As we have seen, many of our respondents note that their dissatisfactions with their particular jobs may be traced to the overall position of part-time workers within the labour force. Many identify part-timers as a convenient and cheap labour reserve. Says a 50-year-old bank teller:

> I know with the banks, when one full-timer leaves, they put a part-timer on her job, to save on benefits. And they will not give them 20 hours, they'll only give them eighteen or nineteen. If you work 20 hours, they have to pay you benefits. That's terrible; I don't know how they get away with it.

Most of these women, whether in non-professional or professional positions, agree that, as part-timers, they are cost-saving assets to their employers. Many are angry about this. But few are able to alter their circumstances at this time.

Whether or not, or for how long, women will accept the dissatisfactions and exploitation inherent in part-time work depends on such factors as domestic pressures, personal needs, satisfactions derived from paid work, and perception of viable alternatives. Not surprisingly, given its disadvantages, our respondents see part-time work as a short-term, life-stage solution. Most expect to be working full-time, in a different organization and in a different position, within the next five or ten years. Their dissatisfactions seem to be manageable when seen in the short run and in light of such pressing considerations as childcare responsibilities.

In considering why they work part-time, some emphasize the lack of available alternatives. Part-time work is presented as a necessity:

> Money in your pocket. Part-time work, I'm sure that's about the only reason anybody ever does it. I certainly don't need it for fulfilment, because I can get that from other areas.

Clearly, with the general decline in real family income experienced by the average Canadian family in the 1980s, women's part-time income is essential (Lindsay, 1986). Despite the conservative bias in the ideology of the family wage, recent escalations in the cost of living, the general erosion of wage standards, and the uncertainty of labour markets – especially within particular industries – have rendered the single pay cheque increasingly inadequate. In fact, wives working part-time or for part of the year contribute approximately 23 percent of family income (Cooke, 1986:13). Structural factors and, most importantly, economic need, are the most significant determinants of mothers' employment decisions (Gordon and Kammeyer, 1980). Women's participation in paid work is affected by many of the same structural problems that affect men: household maintenance, unemployment, economic instability, escalating living costs, health and emergency expenses, and educational costs. Women's paid work options, however, are significantly constrained by the assumption of their responsibilities in the home and by the unequal division of childcare and domestic work.

Our respondents also see their work as necessary in the sense that it ensures their ability to return to full-time work in the future:

> The real reason I'm working part-time right now is to [avoid] this big gap of being at home and not being in the work force. It's just that I plan later to work full-time, and I don't want this gap. In a job application, I can say, "I've worked part-time here" – not ten years ago, or six years ago.

Although professionals are more likely than others to perceive the need to mark time in the labour force, all of our respondents worry about the effects of long terms of absence on their future employment. Women returning to part-time work after having children usually find themselves facing downward mobility – that is, jobs that are lower-paying and more routine than the ones they had before (Hewlett, 1986:85; Sharpe, 1984).

For many, part-time work guarantees a degree of independence. A salesperson, 42, with one child, explains:

> When I was home I would think twice about spending money on myself, because I thought, "I'm not working, I'm not contributing, and we need so many other things." But when I work, I say "I'm putting money in; I deserve it."

Underlying such statements are traditional views: contributions to the household are largely measured in monetary terms; women's unpaid domestic work does not justify their meeting their own needs.

Another common view, espoused by a 40-year-old store clerk with four children, is that part-time work is transitional:

> It isn't for everybody so I don't think I'd say I'd recommend [part-time work]. I certainly wouldn't recommend going from being at home to a full-time job without a transitional period. I think it's a whole lot to go back full-time, but to work into it, that's what I would recommend.

A woman who has spent many years outside the paid labour force may regard her part-time work not as training for the types of jobs she expects later, but as an indispensable way for her – and her family – to adjust to the idea of her participation in the paid labour force. It gives her the opportunity to reorganize family priorities, delegate some household responsibilities to other family members, and study her employment options.

Part-time work appears to many women to be their only viable option for contributing to their families' well-being and for maintaining their labour market status. To listen to their analyses of their limited options, their concerns about managing their families – and, particularly, their frustrations about making childcare arrangements – is to realize that their stated preference for part-time work is constrained by the structure of our society. Their position is circumscribed by an inadequate daycare system, limited employment opportunities, and the lack of enlightened employment policies – such as workplace daycare facilities and programs that would protect parents' labour market positions if they spent prolonged periods in full-time homemaking and childrearing. However this position may be constrained within the realm of limited possibilities, it allows the combination of some of the advantages of participation in the labour force with the satisfactions derived from parenting and homemaking, and is thus the most acceptable option for these women.

Balancing Options?

The common explanation for women's participation in part-time work is that it is undertaken voluntarily and is beneficial. This voluntaristic position assumes that a woman weighs the advantages and disadvantages of available options and then selects the one that best suits her circumstances. Within this framework, women's decisions seem to be shaped by traditional role concepts: women are seen to prefer part-time work because they accept the primacy of motherhood and homemaking.

An alternative explanation, offered here, gives more weight to the ways in which women's options are limited by structural features of society. This interpretation views the availability of part-time work as part of a "circular or domestic trap," which does not alter women's position either in the family or in the paid labour force (Armstrong, 1984:134; Smith, 1983:83; Sharpe, 1984:187). Rather, women's subordinate position is confirmed by the way in which part-time work guarantees the continuation of the double day and the ideology of maternal and family roles, while providing a cheap, largely unorganized and marginal labour reserve.

In the economy, growth in women's job ghettos has often been in part-time work, so that when women enter the labour market the principal kind of work available to them is part-time. Given the present structure of the family, most women in traditional heterosexual relationships are expected to undertake the bulk of domestic and, particularly, childcare duties. As a result, many women do not have the time or energy to take on full-time work on top of their work in the home. The result, once again, is involuntary part-time work.

Attempting to analyze women's participation in part-time work by employing a structuralist explanation alone presents some difficulties. The structuralist view accounts for the overall economic picture, including the increased participation of women in part-time work, despite its drawbacks; the benefit to employers of this marginal work force; and the lack of adequate workplace and childcare policies. Yet this view ignores the possibility that women's part-time work may also, in part, represent an expression of traditional family ideology.

A structuralist explanation of women's part-time work must take into account the personal dilemmas faced by women considering their labour market alternatives and family commitments. Accounting for women's experiences from their own viewpoints requires that we acknowledge how strongly their own values and attitudes as well as those of their reference groups affect their decisions and behaviour. Further, we must not lose sight of the interconnection between the social infrastructure and ideological levels within society (Althusser, 1971:134-135). The recognition of this interrelationship reveals the personal and social conflicts faced by most people. In this framework, the paths people follow, in paid or unpaid labour, on a full- or part-time basis, may be viewed as strategies for dealing with the conflicts created by traditional social values and family structures on the one hand, and real economic pressures, limited opportunities and career options, and inadequate childcare and parental employment policies on the other.

Part-time work represents women's efforts to transcend the limitations of their traditional role in the family while avoiding the double day entailed by full-time paid employment. The women in this study see themselves as striking a delicate balance between the benefits of paid employment (personal autonomy, economic productivity and a measure of independence) and their responsibilities in the family. This balance is not based on, and is not intended to safeguard, a traditional division of domestic labour. In general, these women strive to establish a relatively egalitarian division of domestic chores. The resulting accommodation between paid and domestic work is far from perfect, but may be the best available option for these women in their present life situations.

Part-time women workers appear to be more transitional than traditional. They are caught between two models of woman's role, and are trying to incorporate aspects of each. They have not uncritically accepted the traditional role, nor have they escaped all its limitations. In particular, they seem shortsighted with regard to the possible consequences of their part-time work. Many grew up believing that their husbands would provide their economic support and that their own paid work, if any, would be for pin money. Not having planned to participate in paid work, they now often find themselves in jobs that do not measure up to their expectations. Despite these disappointments, they remain optimistic on many counts – most assume that they will not be working at their present jobs for many years; most believe that they could "get by," or "find a way" if their husbands' financial support were to end; few are concerned that their skills may become obsolete. In fact, they place great faith in traditional structures. Divorce, poverty, and the problems of being a single mother are not connected to their lives at this time or to their decision to work part-time. Yet, in reality, a number of these women, and Canadian women in general, will find themselves completely dependent upon their own economic resources at some point in their lives. Rather than striking a balance, part-time women workers are running a risk with their lives and their futures.

Notes

1. Parts of this chapter are based on an earlier report on the research in progress. See Ann Doris Duffy and Norene Pupo, "Women and Part-Time Work: Looking for Balance Between Home and Work," presented at the Canadian Sociology and Anthropology Association Meetings, Winnipeg, June 1986.

2. Presently in Canada, there is considerable disagreement as to what constitutes part-time work (Wallace, 1983:39-40). *The Labour Force Survey* (LFS) defines part-time work as working less than 30 hours per week. Previously, from 1953 to 1975 the LFS defined part-time work as working less than 35 hours a week. This was revised to 30 hours per week in 1975. In addition to the differences among part-timers with regard to the number of hours worked per week, part-timers may be categorized as permanent or temporary, contractually limited, or seasonal or casual workers.

3. See Chapter One for the definition and discussion of the terms "choice" and "decision-making" as used in this book.

4. Meg Luxton's typology of domestic relations includes: separate spheres and hierarchical relations; separate spheres and co-operative relations; and shared spheres and co-operative relations (1983:31).

5. Blumstein and Schwartz (1983:139) suggest that part-time women workers occupy a middle ground between traditional full-time housewives and women employed full-time in the labour force.

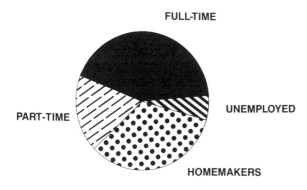

CHAPTER 5

Differing Solutions: Similar Struggles

The women interviewed for this book are strikingly similar in many respects. As interviewers, we expected that there would be many more significant differences than there actually were between employed and non-employed women's accounts of their early dreams, their attitudes towards wage labour and their concerns about children and about spousal relationships. Stereotypical descriptions of women's lives suggest that employed women differ fundamentally from non-employed women in terms of motivation, ambition, fear and guilt. We soon realized that our expectation of differences reflected our own internalization of artificial ideological divisions between work and family. We were associating paid work with men and with social, economic and political significance – in contrast to the unpaid, unworthy and unimportant family work of women. When this false dichotomy is discarded, the commonalities in women's lives become apparent.

All these women are struggling to manage the competing demands of family and paid employment. They have arrived at different, temporary solutions to the dilemma of juggling work and family. Six months or a year from now, some of the full-time homemakers may have joined the ranks of the part-time or full-time paid workers. Factors such as the birth of additional children or serious illness in the family may, for a spell, propel the full-timers into part-time work or full-time homemaking.

Women's work status does not appear to reflect an unwavering commitment to one particular vision of women's lives. Women's paid employment is not necessarily an expression of feminist views, and full-time homemakers are not simply conservative traditionalists. Yet almost all these women accept traditional family ideology. Despite concerns promoted by the media about the death of the family, the basic ideals remain intact: men, as the heads of families, are responsible for economic security; women and children are social, political and economic dependents.

Family ideology continues to prescribe that a certain core of domestic labour is woman's work, regardless of whether a woman engages in wage labour, whether she is economically self-sufficient, or whether she cares for her own children or for those of someone else. The only equivalent assumption for men is their attachment to paid labour. Housework and childcare are not voluntary for married women unless they are able to pay others to perform these tasks. Even then, the norms of good mothering relegate the ultimate responsibility for the family's happiness and well-being, its success or failure, to the mother. For married women, then, although the family may be a source of pleasure, it is never a refuge from the demands of work and society. Rather, it is a site in which the tensions of private and public life overlap.

Many women, then, hold a common set of assumptions about men and women's family roles. Men should devote most of their lives to paid employment; their primary obligation is to "bring home the bacon." This should be combined with extensive secondary responsibilities such as parenting children and supporting the marriage. For women, the script is more ambiguous. Although family relationships, and particularly relationships with children, are assumed to take priority in women's lives, it is seen as undesirable and unnecessary for women to devote their adult lives completely and solely to their husbands and children. This modern female gender role reflects major societal changes, particularly those that have occurred since the 1950s – including the heightened demand for women workers, escalating divorce rates and the increasing prevalence of families headed by single mothers. Almost all the women interviewed here are attempting to negotiate these new, contradictory role requirements.

Today, many women in Canada are juggling the conflicting demands of family and work. Most have resolved periods of intense conflict by moving in and out of the labour force and by taking part-time employment. As a result, women typically work full-time prior to marriage and motherhood. They withdraw from paid employment during their children's infancy. After one (or several) long (or short) break(s), they return to either part-time or full-time employment (Burch, 1985). Part-time employment is particularly popular when there are still young children at home (Statistics Canada, 1985). The overall trend is for more and more women to combine marriage, family, and paid work; to spend more of their adult lives in paid employment; and to take fewer and shorter breaks from work (Burch, 1985).

Viewed in this context, many of women interviewed here are simply at different phases of their lives. Those who are in the midst of such intense domestic obligations as the rearing of young children, who do not have access to such solutions as reliable daycare and paid or unpaid help with domestic chores, who are not subject to extreme financial need and who lack desireable or viable employment opportunities will be pushed into the home. When these pressures shift – when daycare and employment become available, when children enter school, when financial need intensifies – the same women will be propelled into paid employment.

Many share the idea that women ought to nurture and support their families but, at some point in their lives, should do something more than housework and childcare. Many of the differences between these women are created by such conditions as the availability of daycare, opportunities for paid work, rates of inflation and housing costs, as well as the vagaries of fate, such as children's health. Systemic social factors (class, age, race, ethnicity) intersect with and reinforce these differences. Still, it is important to recognize the degree to which many Canadian women are confronting similar issues, and are faced with similar, flawed solutions.

Coping with Flawed Alternatives
No solution to the problem of balancing work and family is entirely satisfactory. Regardless of what stance women take vis-à-vis paid employment, they are going to pay a penalty. If we assume that women have a choice, then they are forced to choose between seriously flawed alternatives. Each of the women we interviewed had to work out strategies to cope with the drawbacks of her particular life situation.

Housework is a solo activity, for example, from which both isolation and gratification derive. As a labour of love, caring for and serving others provides housewives with an often satisfying way to form intimate relationships. For many women, having and rearing children is their only opportunity to form loving, enduring and empowering relationships with others. Women's organization of their lives and creative energies to accommodate the needs of others provides satisfaction for husbands and children. But it often leaves homemakers feeling alone, dependent and unfulfilled. Emotionally, socially and economically dependent, the housewife may lose her self-esteem, personal identity and financial security. Further, when women re-enter the paid labour force, they frequently find that their time-out in the home, far from being valued by potential employers, is actually a serious impediment to occupational continuity and advancement.

Part-time workers, with their feet in two worlds, both adhere to traditional family ideology and gain a sense of self-worth and independence from paid labour. Many of these women resolve the balancing problem experienced by all employed mothers by giving higher priority to family concerns than to employment demands. Given the difficulty of carrying out two jobs and the lack of social support for doing so, their decision may seem like a reasonable compromise. Opting for fewer working hours and a relatively low level of career commitment may satisfy women's need for money, stimulation and social support. Unfortunately, it also guarantees their continued ghettoization in low-paying, low-status job markets with few opportunities for training or advancement.

Of all the women interviewed, the mothers who work full-time for pay most clearly reveal the pressures women experience in combining employment and motherhood. Hypothetically, mothers are free, once their children go to school, to pursue employment. But in fact, their freedom is limited to certain hours of the day and times of the year. This restricts occupational choices (Gittens, 1985). Time pressures are compounded by the expectation of husbands and children that, regardless of women's outside activities, they will put their families first. These ideological assumptions push the weight of family guilt onto women. If family problems arise – if the children are deviant, if husbands have affairs – then wives perceive the failure as personal, rather than societal. Employed mothers articulate this guilt in various ways: perhaps they should be spending more time helping their children with homework; perhaps they should be putting more energy into their marriages. Full-time employment necessarily entails less time spent in mothering and domestic activities. The prevailing ideology encourages women to assume responsibility and blame for any problems they encounter in shouldering family and work responsibilities.

Although mothers who work full-time for pay have more opportunity than those who work part-time to compete in the job market for non-exploitative work that will pay adequately and provide job satisfaction, the balancing of full-time wage and domestic labour exacts a personal price. All these women feel stressed from attempting to maintain a traditional maternal role and simultaneously engage in full-time employment. Their individual coping strategies, on some level, reflect an admission of their deviation from family ideology. Rather than attempting to alter family ideals by pressing for structural alterations in society, these women reinforce traditional stereotypes by attempting to "do it all." Several studies have suggested that employed mothers are physically and emotionally happier, have higher self-esteem and feel less isolated than non-employed mothers, regardless of how low-status and low-paying their jobs are. But this gain is offset by their constant lack of sufficient time and energy to meet personal, work and family demands. Full-time homemakers enjoy considerable autonomy and freedom, and usually pleasure, in their work, which mothers who work full-time for pay may be too rushed to experience.

Women work hard to manage the drawbacks of their particular life situations. Homemakers participate in volunteer activities to reduce domestic isolation; full-time and part-time workers try to set aside personal time to relax. Those who can afford it hire domestic and childcare help; others urge their husbands and children to become more involved in domestic chores, and make plans for more fulfilling and balanced lives. Women's strategies for resisting the pressures and constraints of home and workplace help them cope – or, at least, get by. But they do not resolve the fundamental sense of powerlessness that so often seems to permeate women's lives.

From Drifting to Ambivalence: Ideology and Powerlessness
In 1959, C. Wright Mills (1959:3) commented on the pervasive feelings of entrapment in modern society:

> Nowadays men [and women] often feel that their private lives are a series of traps. They sense that within their everyday worlds, they cannot overcome their troubles, and in this feeling, they are often quite correct: What ordinary men [and women] are directly aware of and what they try to do are bounded by the private orbits in which they live; their visions and their powers are limited to the close-up scenes of job, family, neighbourhood; in other milieux, they move vicariously and remain spectators. And the more aware they become, however vaguely, of ambitions and of threats which transcend their immediate locales, the more trapped they seem to feel.

Many of the women interviewed here seem to experience this powerlessness. Early in life, they often drift along, without clear plans or goals – waiting, in effect, for life to happen to them. Life is assumed to include marriage and motherhood. Not to marry and / or not to have children is, for most, an unthinkable option. As women mature, their activities are often characterized by uncertainty and ambivalence. Encouraged by traditional socialization to be passive and to devote their energies to others, they often find it difficult to be purposeful and focused. Frequently, any plans they may have are short-term and contingent on the activities or inclinations of others ("when my children go to school"; "because my husband got a new job").

In order to acquire power in their public and private lives, women would have to have the resources and opportunities to freely decide between clear alternatives. Most women do not. In many respects, their decisions are made for them by the economy and the state. The major features of most women's lives are the products of external forces, not the women's personal predilections. For example, it is not the case that, commencing about 1950, more and more married women simply chose to devote more of their adult lives to paid employment. Rather, such factors as economic pressures, the increasing demand for women workers and the availability of birth control constructed a social reality in which most mothers now take it for granted that they must devote some portion of their adult lives to wage labour. Trapped within this reality, women attempt in a variety of ways to make their lives as rewarding and manageable as possible.

But family ideology and traditional gender roles tend to mask this reality from both men and women, by translating social and political problems into personal and individual ones, thus changing political anger into individual guilt and malaise (Gittens, 1985:165). Women working full-time in the paid labour force may feel guilty about not always being able to fulfill their responsibilities as wives and mothers. Typically, they do not direct their anger towards, or challenge, a political and social order that expects them to carry an unmanageable burden of work. Rather, they blame themselves ("I should be more efficient"; "I need to spend more time with the kids") and work out personal solutions ("I'll start keeping lists"; "I'll set aside Saturday afternoons to be with the kids"). The ideologies of gender and of the family encourage women's preoccupation with personal problems and personal solutions, and obscure political issues and public policy.

At present, women are inadvertently perpetuating their entrapment by taking on ever greater amounts of work, managing ever more contradictory demands on their time, and accepting ever greater stress in their day-to-day lives. Women can only effectively challenge current notions of their role if they urge the rethinking of family, economic and gender systems. Clearly, for twentieth-century Canadian women, combining wage and domestic labour, either daily or in the course of their lives, is a major social problem. Even though various career paths are apparently open to women, as long as society rigidly maintains women's responsibility for the family, these options will confront young women as agonizing alternatives. Only through developing a critical social awareness and taking social action can women (and men) challenge their lack of real choices (Czerny and Swift, 1988).

Struggling Towards Choices

Our society's new questioning of women's (and men's) roles in the family and the workplace must be intensified. Each of the suggestions that follow may be flawed. But by presenting alternatives, we are attempting to provide women (and men) with a full range of life choices that will optimize personal and social satisfaction. Our interviews suggest that women find it hard to cope with the current arrangement of family and work. This suggests that the nature of paid employment and the structure of the family ought to be scrutinized to provide a greater variety of choices for women (and men).

Part-time work should not penalize women, but rather should be secure and permanent, and should offer pro-rated benefits. Extended paternity leave policies should be considered as part of our serious rethinking of the entire childcare issue. In general, both social attitudes and employment structures should allow men more opportunity to take on a major parenting role and greater participation in the domestic realm. Finally, paid employment could be structurally altered to provide more opportunities for job-sharing. Job flexibility in general, including job-sharing, flex-time and compressed work-weeks, is not incompatible with productivity, nor need it interfere with the efficient functioning of institutions. Some corporations have already begun to institute these changes, recognizing that contented workers are ultimately more productive. It is the resistance to changing definitions of work, and the ignorance of alternatives, that constrain the consideration of structural strategies.

The modern women's movement has pressed for increased state involvement in women's issues by demanding national daycare, abortion on demand and no-fault divorce. It cannot be assumed, however, that the state acts in women's best interest (Pupo, 1988). Changes in social legislation present hazards for women unless accompanied by a push for equal wages and for the end of gender discrimination (Heitlinger, 1987). Since state policies have, to date, been heavily influenced by patriarchal ideology, state involvement is not an unequivocal panacea for women's problems. Women and men must re-evaluate group activities and seek nonbureaucratic, manageable alternatives. Perhaps we should rethink the proposals put forward in the 1860s by American feminists for "co-operative housekeeping," in which domestic labour and childcare would be provided communally (Hayden, 1981). Certainly, communities and neighbourhood groups could begin by creating a range of parent co-operative daycare services that would provide full-time homemakers with days off each week, and also provide full-time care for employed mothers.

As industrial capitalism advances in the West, we are increasingly dominated by the economic order. Our identities are primarily defined by our work. Our happiness and self-esteem is often measured in relation to work activities. And our family lives are constantly wrapped around our work demands. The challenge of the 1990s will be to balance this tendency against the simultaneous pressure for rewarding, satisfying and mutually supportive personal relationships. In order to achieve individual and social harmony, women and men together must look closely at work and the family, and consider rethinking both.

Bibliography

Akyeampong, Ernest, 1986. "Involuntary Part-Time Employment in Canada, 1975-85," in Statistics Canada, *The Labour Force Survey*, Catalogue 71-001 (December).

Akyeampong, Ernest, 1987. "Involuntary Part-Time Employment in Canada, 1975-1986," *Canadian Social Trends*, Autumn:26-29.

Althusser, Louis, 1971. "Ideology and Ideological State Apparatuses (Notes Towards an Investigation)," in *Lenin, Philosophy and Other Essays*. New York: Monthly Review Press.

Andre, Rae, 1981. *Homemakers: The Forgotten Workers*. Chicago: The University of Chicago Press.

Archibald, Kathleen, 1973. *Sex and the Public Service*. Ottawa: Information Canada.

Archibald, Peter, 1978. *Social Psychology as Political Economy*. Toronto: McGraw-Hill Ryerson.

Armstrong, Pat, 1984. *Labour Pains: Women's Work in Crisis*. Toronto: The Women's Press.

Armstrong, Pat and Hugh Armstrong, 1983. *A Working Majority*. Ottawa: Canadian Advisory Council on the Status of Women.

Armstrong, Pat and Hugh Armstrong, 1984. *The Double Ghetto*. Revised Edition. Toronto: McClelland and Stewart.

Armstrong, Pat and Hugh Armstrong, 1988. "Women, Family and Economy," in N. Mandell and A. Duffy, (eds.), *Re-constructing the Canadian Family*. Toronto: Butterworths.

Baker, Maureen, 1985. "What Will Tomorrow Bring ...?" A Study of the Aspirations of Adolescent Women. Ottawa: Canadian Advisory Council on the Status of Women.

Baruch, Grace, Rosalind Barnett and Caryl Rivers, 1983. *Lifeprints: New Patterns of Love and Work for Today's Women.* New York: New American Library.

Beechey, Veronica and Tessa Perkins, 1987. *A Matter of Hours: Women, Part-Time Work and the Labour Market.* Minneapolis: University of Minnesota Press.

Berk, Sarah, 1985. *The Gender Factory: The Appointment of Work in American Households.* New York: Plenum.

Bernardo, Donna H., Constance L. Shehan and Gerald R. Leslie, 1987. "A Resident of Tradition: Jobs, Careers and Spouses' Time in Housework," *Journal of Marriage and the Family,* 49:381-390.

Bibby, Reginald W. and Donald C. Posterski, 1985. *The Emerging Generation.* Toronto: Irwin Publishing.

Bird, Florence, 1970. *Report of the Royal Commission on the Status of Women in Canada.* Ottawa: Minister of Supply and Services.

Blumstein, Philip and Pepper Schwartz, 1983. *American Couples.* New York: William Morrow.

Bose, Christine, 1980. "Social Status of the Homemaker," in Sarah F. Berk, (ed.), *Women and Household Labor.* Beverly Hills: Sage Publications.

Boyd, Monica, 1981. "English-Canadian and French-Canadian Attitudes Toward Women: Results of the Canadian Gallup Polls," in George Kurian and Ratna Ghosh, (eds.), *Women in the Family and the Economy.* Westport, Connecticut: Greenwood Press.

Boyd, Monica, 1988. "Changing Canadian Family Forms: Issues for Women," in N. Mandell and A. Duffy, (eds.), *Reconstructing the Canadian Family.* Toronto: Butterworths.

Burch, Thomas K., 1985. *Family History Survey Preliminary Findings.* Ottawa: Minister of Supply and Services.

Canadian Congress for Learning Opportunities for Women, 1986. *Decade of Promise.* Toronto.

Canadian Mental Health Association, 1987. *Women and Mental Health* in Canada.

Chatelaine, March, 1988. "The Changing Canadian Woman," 77ff.

Coates, Mary Lou, 1988. *Part-Time Employment: Labour Market Flexibility and Equity Issues.* Kingston: Industrial Relations Centre, Queen's University.

Cogle, Francis L. and Grace E. Tasker, 1982. "Children and Housework," *Family Relations,* 395-399.

Coleman, Lerita M. and Toni C. Antonucci, 1985. "Impact of Work on

Women at Midlife," in Brent C. Miller and David H. Olson, (eds.), *Family Studies Review Yearbook 3*. Beverly Hills: Sage Publications.

Connelly, M. Patricia and Linda Christiansen-Ruffman, 1987. "Women's Problems: Private Troubles or Public Issues?" in E.D. Salaman and B.W. Robinson, (eds.), *Gender Roles: Doing What Comes Naturally*. Toronto: Methuen.

Cook, Judith A. and Mary M. Fonow, 1986. "Knowledge and Women's Interests: Issues of Epistemology and Methodology in Feminist Sociological Research," *Sociological Inquiry,* 56 (Winter).

Cooke, Katie, 1986. *Report of The Task Force on Child Care*. Ottawa: Status of Women Canada.

Coser, Lewis, 1974. *Greedy Institutions: Patterns of Undivided Commitment*. New York: Free Press.

Cowan, Ruth Schwartz, 1983. *More Work for Mother*. New York: Basic Books.

Crouter, Ann C., 1984. "Spillover From Family to Work: The Neglected Side of the Work / Family Interface," *Human Relations,* 378:6:425-442.

Czerny, Michael and Jamie Swift, 1988. *Getting Started: On Social Analysis in Canada*. Second Edition. Toronto: Between the Lines.

D'Arcy, Carl and C.M. Siddique, 1985. "Marital Status and Psychological Well-Being: A Cross-National Comparative Analysis," *International Journal of Comparative Sociology,* 26:3-4:149-166.

Duffy, Ann Doris and Norene Pupo, 1986. "Women and Part-Time Work: Looking for Balance Between Home and 'Work'". Unpublished. Presented at the Canadian Sociology and Anthropology Associations Meetings, Winnipeg.

Dyk, Patricia A.H., 1987. "Graduate Student Management of Family and Academic Roles," *Family Relations,* 36:329-332.

Eagly, Alice H. and Valerie J. Steffen, 1986. "Gender Stereotypes, Occupational Roles, and Beliefs about Part-Time Employees," *Psychology of Women Quarterly,* 10:252-262.

Ehrenreich, Barbara and Deirdre English, 1978. *For Her Own Good*. Garden City, New York: Anchor Books.

Eichler, Margrit, 1977. "The Prestige of the Occupation Housewife," in P. Marchak, (ed.), *The Working Sexes*. Vancouver: Institute of Industrial Relations, U.B.C.

Ferguson, Kathy, 1984. *The Feminist Case Against Bureaucracy*. Philadelphia: Temple University Press.

Ferree, Myra Marx, 1976. "Working-Class Jobs: Housework and Paid Work as Sources of Satisfaction," *Social Problems,* 23:431-441.

Ferree, Myra Marx, 1984. "Class, Housework, and Happiness: Women's Work and Life Satisfaction," *Sex Roles* 2:11,12:1057-1074.

Finch, Janet, 1983. *Married to the Job: Wives' Incorporation in Men's Work.* London: George Allen and Unwin.

Floge, Liliane, 1985. "The Dynamics of Child-Care Use and Some Implications for Women's Employment," *Journal of Marriage and the Family* 47:1:143-154.

Fox, Bonnie, 1980. (ed.), *Hidden in the Household.* Toronto: The Women's Press.

Fox, Mary Frank and Sharlene Hesse-Biber, 1984. *Women at Work.* Palo Alto, California: Mayfield.

Freudiger, Patricia, 1983. "Life Satisfaction Among Three Categories of Married Women," *Journal of Marriage and the Family,* 45:1:213-219.

Friedan, Betty, 1963. *The Feminine Mystique.* New York: Dell Publishing.

Genevie, Louis and Eva Margolies, 1987. *The Motherhood Report: How Women Feel About Being Mothers.* New York: Macmillan.

Gerson, Kathleen, 1985. *Hard Choices: How Women Decide About Work, Career, and Motherhood.* Berkeley: University of California Press.

Gilligan, Carol, 1982. *In a Different Voice.* Cambridge, Massachusetts: Harvard University Press.

Gittens, Diana, 1985. *The Family in Question.* London: Macmillan.

Gordon, Henry A. and Kenneth C.W. Kammeyer, 1980. "The Gainful Employment of Women With Small Children," *Journal of Marriage and The Family,* May.

Gramling, Robert and Craig Forsyth, 1987. "Work Scheduling and Family Interaction," *Journal of Family Issues,* 8:2:173-175.

Greenhaus, Jeffrey H. and Nicholas J. Beutell, 1985. "Sources of Conflict Between Work and Family Roles," *Academy of Management Review,* 10 (January).

Greenstein, Theodore N., 1986. "Social-Psychological Factors in Perinatal Labor-Force Participation," *Journal of Marriage and the Family,* 48:3:565-571.

Greer, Germaine, 1984. *Sex and Destiny.* London: Secker and Warburg.

Hayden, Dolores, 1981. *The Grand Domestic Revolution: A History of Feminist Designs for American Homes, Neighborhoods, and Cities.* Cambridge, Mass.: MIT Press.

Heitlinger, Alena, 1987. "Maternity Leaves, Protective Legislation, and Sex Equality: Eastern European and Canadian Perspectives," in H. Maroney and M. Luxton, (eds.), *Feminism and Political Economy.* Toronto: Methuen.

Hertz, Rosanna, 1986. *More Equal Than Others: Women and Men in Dual-Career Marriages.* Berkeley, California: University of California Press.

Hewlett, Sylvia Ann, 1986. *A Lesser Life: The Myth of Women's Liberation in America.* New York: William Morrow.

Hochschild, Arlie, 1975. "The Sociology of Feeling and Emotion: Selected Possibilities," in Marcia Millman and Rosabeth Moss Kanter, (eds.), *Another Voice*. New York: Anchor.

Hock, Ellen, M. Therese Gnezda and Susan L. McBride, 1984. "Mothers of Infants: Attitudes Towards Employment and Motherhood Following Birth of the First Child," *Journal of Marriage and the Family*, 46:2:425-431.

Johnson, Laura C. and Rona Abramovitch, 1987. "Rush Hours: A New Look at Parental Employment Patterns," *Social Infopac*, 6:4:1-4.

Jones, Ethel B. and James E. Long, 1979. "Part-Week Work and Human Capital Investment By Married Women," *Journal of Human Resources*, 14:4:563-78.

Kalmuss, Debra S. and Murray A. Straus, 1982. "Wife's Marital Dependency and Wife Abuse," *Journal of Marriage and the Family*, 44:1:277-286.

Kanter, Rosabeth Moss, 1977. *Men and Women of the Corporation*. New York: Basic.

Katz, Michael B., 1975. *The People of Hamilton, Canada West*. Cambridge, Massachusetts: Harvard University Press.

Kervin, John, 1983. "The Problems of Part-Time Work: An Exploratory Study," Unpublished study for the Wallace Commission.

Kessler, R.C. and J.A. McRae, 1982. "The Effect of Wives' Employment on the Mental Health of Maried Men and Women," *American Sociological Review*, 47:216-227.

Kome, Penney, 1982. *Somebody Has To Do It*. Toronto: McClelland and Stewart.

Levesque, Jean Marc, 1987. "The Growth of Part-Time Work in a Changing Industrial Environment," *The Labour Force Survey*, Catalogue 71-001, May.

Levine, Helen, 1983. "The Power Politics of Motherhood," in J. Turner and L. Emery, (eds.), *Perspectives on Women in the 1980s*. Winnipeg: The University of Winnipeg Press.

Lindsay, Colin, 1986. "The Decline of Real Family Income, 1980 to 1984," *Canadian Social Trends*, Winter:15-17.

Long, James E. and Ethel B. Jones, 1980. "Part-Week Work By Married Women," *Southern Economic Journal*, 46:716-725.

Long, James E. and Ethel B. Jones, 1981. "Married Women in Part-Time Employment," *Industrial and Labour Relations Review*, 34:3:413-425.

Lowe, Graham S and H. Krahn, 1985. "Where Wives Work: The Relative Effects of Situational and Attitudinal Factors," *Canadian Journal of Sociology*, 10:1:1-22.

Luxton, Meg, 1980. *More Than a Labour of Love*. Toronto: The Women's Press.

Luxton, Meg, 1983. "Two Hands for the Clock: Changing Patterns in the Gendered Division of Labour," *Studies in Political Economy*, 10.

Luxton, Meg, 1987. "Time for Myself: Women's Work and The 'Fight for Shorter Hours,'" in Heather Jon Maroney and Meg Luxton, (eds.), *Feminism and Political Economy*, Toronto: Methuen.

MacLeod, Linda, 1980. *Wife Battering in Canada: The Vicious Circle*. Ottawa: Canadian Advisory Council on the Status of Women.

MacLeod, Linda, 1987. *Battered But Not Beaten ... Preventing Wife Battering in Canada*. Ottawa: Canadian Advisory Council on the Status of Women.

Mandell, Nancy, 1987. "The Family," in M. Michael Rosenberg, William Shaffir, Allan Turowitz and Morton Weinfeld, (eds.), *An Introduction to Sociology*. Second Edition. Toronto: Methuen.

Mandell, Nancy, 1989. "Marital Roles in Transition," in K. Ishwaran, (ed.), *The Family and Marriage: A Cross-Cultural Introduction*. Toronto: Hall and Thompson.

Marsden, Lorna, 1981. "The Labour Force is an Ideological Structure," *Atlantis*, 7 (Fall):57-64.

Martin, Jean and Ceridwen Roberts, 1984. *Women and Employment: A Lifetime Perspective*. London: Her Majesty's Stationery Office.

Matthews, Glenna, 1987. *Just a Housewife*. New York: Oxford University Press.

Maynard, Rona, 1988. "The Changing Canadian Woman," *Chatelaine*, 61 (March):81.

McKie, D.C., B. Prentice and P. Reed, 1983. *Divorce: Law and the Family in Canada*. Ottawa: Minister of Supply and Services.

Michelson, William, 1985. *From Sun to Sun: Daily Obligations and Community Structure in the Lives of Employed Women and Their Families*. New Jersey: Rowman and Allanheld.

Miller, Beatrice J., 1988. "Unmasking the Labour Board: The Big Chill Organizing Part-Timers," *Our Times*, 7:1, 28-31.

Miller, Brent C. and Judith A. Myers-Walls, 1983. "Parenthood: Stresses and Coping Strategies," in Charles R. Figley and Hamilton I. McCubbin, (eds.), *Stress and the Family*. New York: Brunner / Mazel.

Miller, Jean Baker, 1976. *Toward a New Psychology of Women*. Boston: Beacon Press.

Mills, C. Wright, 1959. *The Sociological Imagination*. London: Oxford University Press.

Mitchell, Juliet, 1966. *Woman's Estate*. Baltimore, Maryland: Penguin Books.

Moore, H.A., 1985. "Job Satisfaction and Women's Spheres of Work," *Sex Roles*, 13:663-678.

National Council on Welfare, 1988. *Poverty Profile*. Ottawa: Minister of Supply and Services.

Oakley, Ann, 1974. *Woman's Work The Housewife, Past and Present*. New York: Pantheon Books.

Oakley, Ann, 1981. "Interviewing Women: A Contradiction in Terms," in Helen Roberts, (ed.), *Doing Feminist Research*. London: Routledge and Kegan Paul.

O'Donnell, Lydia N., 1985. *The Unheralded Majority*. Lexington, Massachusetts: Lexington Books.

Paloma, Margaret M. and T. Neil Garland, 1971. "The Married Professional Woman: A Study in the Tolerance of Domestication," *Journal of Marriage and the Family* 33:3:531-540.

Phillips, Paul and Erin Phillips, 1983. *Women and Work*. Toronto: James Lorimer and Company, Publishers.

Pleck, Joseph, G.L. Staines and L. Long, 1980. "Conflicts Between Work and Family Life," *Monthly Labor Review*, 103:3:29-32.

Popenoe, David, 1987. "Beyond the Nuclear Family: A Statistical Portrait of the Changing Family in Sweden," *Journal of Marriage and the Family*, 49:1:173-183.

Presser, Harriet B., 1986. "Shift Work Among American Women and Child Care," *Journal of Marriage and The Family*, 48:3:551-63.

Pupo, Norene, 1988. "Preserving Patriarchy: Women, The Family and the State," in N. Mandell and A. Duffy, (eds.), *Reconstructing the Canadian Family*. Toronto: Butterworths.

Pupo, Norene and Ann Duffy, 1987. "Interviewer Effects, Gender Differences and Power: A Reiteration of Some Feminist Methodological Concerns". Unpublished. Presented at the Qualitative Research Conference, Hamilton.

Rapoport, Rhona and Robert N. Rapoport, 1976. *Dual-Career Families Re-examined: New Integrations of Work and Family*. New York: Harper and Row, 1976.

Reynaud, Emmaneul, 1983. *Holy Virility: Social Construction of Masculinity*. London: Pluto Press.

Rinehart, James W., 1984. "Contradictions of Work-Related Attitudes and Behaviour: An Interpretation," in G.S. Lowe and H.J. Krahn, (eds.), *Working Canadians*, Toronto: Methuen.

Rinehart, James W., 1987. *The Tyranny of Work*. Second edition. Toronto: Harcourt, Brace and Jovanovich.

Roberts, Wayne, 1976. *Honest Womanhood*. Toronto: New Hogtown Press.

Robinson, Patricia, 1986. *Women's Work Interruptions*. Ottawa: Minister of Supply and Services.

Rosenthal, Caroline, 1982. "Family Responsibilities and Concerns: A Perspective on the Lives of Middle-Aged Women," *Resources for Feminist Research.*

Roy, Maria, 1980. (ed.), *The Abusive Partner: An Analysis of Domestic Bettering.* New York: Van Nostrand Reinhold.

Rubin, Lillian, 1976. *Worlds of Pain: Life in the Working Class Family.* New York: Basic.

Schafer, Robert B. and Patricia M. Keith, 1984. "Equity in Marital Roles Across the Family Life Cycle," in David H. Olson and Brent C. Miller, (eds.), *Family Studies Review Yearbook 2.* Beverly Hills: Sage Publications.

Sharpe, Sue, 1984. *Double Identity: The Lives of Working Mothers.* Harmondsworth: Penguin Books.

Simpson, Ida Harper and Paula England, 1983. "Conjugal Work Roles and Marital Solidarity," in David H. Olson and Brent C. Miller, (eds.), *Family Studies Review Yearbook 1.* Beverly Hills: Sage Publications.

Sinclair, Deborah, 1985. *Understanding Wife Assault.* Toronto: Ontario Government.

Skinner, Denise, 1984. "Dual-Career Family Stress and Coping: A Literature Review," in Patricia Voydanoff, (ed.), *Work and Family.* Palo Alto: Mayfield.

Smith, Dorothy, 1974. "Women's Perspective as a Radical Critique of Sociology," *Sociological Inquiry,* 44:1, 1974.

Smith, Vicki, 1983. "The Circular Trap: Women and Part-Time Work," *Berkeley Journal of Sociology,* XXVII:1-17.

Staines, Graham L. and Joseph H. Pleck, 1983. *The Impact of Work Schedules on the Family.* The Institute for Social Research, The University of Michigan.

Statistics Canada, 1984. *The Elderly in Canada.* Ottawa: Minister of Supply and Services.

Statistics Canada, 1984a. *Urban Growth in Canada.* Ottawa: Minister of Supply and Services.

Statistics Canada, 1985. *Women in Canada: A Statistical Report.* Ottawa: Minister of Supply and Services Canada.

Statistics Canada, 1987. *The Labour Force Survey.* January. Ottawa: Minister of Supply and Services.

Statistics Canada, 1987a. *The Labour Force Survey.* December. Ottawa: Minister of Supply and Services.

Statistics Canada, 1988. *The Labour Force Survey.* May. Ottawa: Minister of Supply and Services.

Stokes, Joseph P. and Judith S. Peyton, 1986. "Attitudinal Differences

Between Full-time Homemakers and Women Who Work Outside the Home," *Sex Roles*, 15:5,6:299-310.

Swinamer, J.L., 1986. "The Value of Household Work in Canada," *Canadian Social Trends*. Autumn:42.

The Activist, 1975. 15:1,2.

Waite, Linda J., Gus W. Haggstrom and David E. Kanouse, 1985. "Change in the Employment Activities of New Parents," *American Sociological Review*, 50:263-272.

Walker, Lenore, 1979. *The Battered Woman*. New York: Harper and Row.

Wallace, Joan, 1983. *Part-Time Work in Canada*. Ottawa: Ministry of Supply and Services.

Weeks, Wendy, 1980. "Part-Time Work: The Business View on Second-Class Jobs for Housewives and Mothers," *Atlantis*, 5:2:69-88.

White, Julie, 1983. *Women and Part-Time Work*. Ottawa: Ministry of Supply and Services.

White, Lynn K. and David B. Brinkerhoff, 1981. "Children's Work in the Family: Its Significance and Meaning," *Journal of Marriage and the Family*, 43:789-798.

Wilson, S.J., 1986. *Women, the Family and the Economy*. Second edition. Toronto: McGraw-Hill Ryerson.

Woodsworth, E. *et al.*, 1987. *It's Time Women Speak Out*. Vancouver: Housewives in Training and Research.

Yeandle, Susan, 1984. *Women's Working Lives: Patterns and Strategies*. London: Tavistock Publications.

The Network Basics Series

T.W. Acheson, David Frank, James Frost: *Industrialization and Underdevelopment in the Maritimes, 1880-1930*

Pat Armstrong et al: *Feminist Marxism or Marxist Feminism: A Debate*

Howard Buchbinder et al: *Who's On Top: The Politics of Heterosexuality*

Varda Burstyn and Dorothy Smith: *Women, Class, Family and the State*; introduction by Roxana Ng

Marjorie Cohen: *Free Trade and the Future of Women's Work: Manufacturing and Service Industries*

Duffy, Mandell, Pupo: *Few Choices: Women, Work and Home*

Lesley Harman: *When a Hostel Becomes a Home: Experiences of Women*

Dany Lacombe: *Ideology and Public Policy*

David Livingstone: *Social Crisis and Schooling*

Graham Lowe and Herb Northcott: *Under Pressure: a Study of Job Stress*

Meg Luxton and Harriet Rosenberg: *Through the Kitchen Window: The Politics of Home and Family*

Janice Newson, Howard Buchbinder: *The University Means Business*

Roxana Ng: *The Politics of Community Services*

Leo Panitch and Don Swartz: *The Assault on Trade Union Freedoms* (2nd. ed.)

Henry Veltmeyer: *The Canadian Class Structure*

Henry Veltmeyer: *Canadian Corporate Power*

Robert White: *Law, Capitalism and the Right to Work*

Garamond Press
67A Portland Street
Toronto, Ontario M5V 2M9
(416) 597-0246